Encounters

with

Nigel

Encounters with Nigel
Celebrating the life of Nigel Jenkins

Edited by Jon Gower

with a Foreword by Ali Anwar

The Poetry Foundation
Y Sefydliad Barddoniaeth

Cover photograph of Nigel Jenkins © Philip Griffiths
(NB:Design, Llangennith) 2014.

ISBN: 978-0-9927560-4-8

Acknowledgement is due to Nigel Jenkins' literary executors, *Planet: The Welsh Internationalist*, *Wales Arts Review* and to the Institute of Welsh Affairs who first published some of the tributes contained herein.

Typeset and designed by Dafydd Prys
Printed in Wales by Gwasg Gomer, Llandysul

Published by The H'mm Foundation, Grove Extension – Room 426, Swansea University, Singleton Park, Swansea SA2 8PP

Contents

Foreword

Ali Anwar – Yes Nigel, your company is hugely missed

It was Tuesday, 9 February, 2014, a rainy cold evening in Cardiff; I drove to Pontcanna to pick up Jon Gower from his house, and then drive to Swansea. Not to stay with our dearest friend Nigel Jenkins, and to share some jokes and a few glasses of red wine. No, not this time. This time it was to attend his funeral the following day at St Mary's Church, Pennard, Gower. How terribly sad.

We stayed the night in Mumbles, a few minutes' walk from Nigel's house in Chapel Street. For supper we went to an Indian restaurant on Newton Road where, ironically, I worked as a dish washer in the late 1970s, after I'd arrived from Baghdad. It was the period when I encountered Nigel in Swansea for the first time.

Yes, I have known Nigel for over thirty years, with a few interruptions. I didn't meet him often during the 1980s and somehow he managed to acquire a police record for refusing to pay a fine after a CND protest outside the American airbase in Brawdy, Pembrokeshire, and we rarely met when he was working for ten years on his *Encyclopaedia of Wales*.

Our first meeting was rather disappointing, we were at a house of Chilean refugees in the Sketty area of Swansea. We, the foreigners, were having a conversation, in pigeon English, about how lovely Swansea was and how romantic the name is, with the words Swan and Sea.

The long-haired Bohemian-looking Nigel said 'Oh, Swansea is named after a Viking called Sweyn who established a settlement on the river Tawe'. We all looked at each other and said *what Vikings*? *In Swansea*? One Chilean asked if there was any evidence of the Viking invaders chasing the Welsh girls in Mumbles! That really amused Nigel.

My subsequent encounters with Nigel were not so frequent, mostly at a pub with a fireplace in Mumbles, probably the old White Rose. I met him with Harry Stratton, who knew Nigel well. I met Harry by pure coincidence. He was a retired taxi driver who lived in Gower. He volunteered to join the International Brigade to fight in the Spanish civil war 1936-39. He published a fascinating book called *To Anti Fascism By Taxi*. The flow of conversations and Harry's stories were very memorable.

Then I saw more of Nigel when I moved to Hanover Street to share a flat with a Chilean Refugee called Leandro who was studying at Swansea University. Nigel was very interested in international politics. In the early eighties he helped the Chilean and Iraqi students living in Swansea with their human rights campaigns. As a journalist he helped in organising press releases, contacting the media and taking part in public meetings and events.

Whenever I visited him, he always greeted me with his genuine warmth, *'Croeso, mae lle yn y tafarn'* (there is a room at the inn) he used to say, laughing. (There is a long story behind this, but no space to tell.) At his wooden bungalow in Mumbles, where he used to brew... not sure what, you helped yourself directly from the barrel. You only needed a small amount to get somewhat inebriated. It wasn't made for the faint hearted...

I feel so privileged that Nigel wrote an essay about me: 'The H'mm Foundation' which was published in *Planet* magazine in January 2012. Nigel's original title was 'Ali and the Forty Bards'. He only wrote essays about a few people such as John Cale, John Tripp and Tony Conran. He took an interest in my story, as 'an accidental incomer' to his beloved Wales and someone who became a 'settler' in Swansea.

The bit that made him laugh most was when I used to report, monthly, to the 'Aliens Department' at the Swansea Central Police Station. I used to go with my friend Araf, who helped with translation. Once an officer told us, 'You have Welsh names, *Araf* means Slow and *Anwar* means uncivilised! But don't be disheartened about being called an alien, Prince Philip is an alien.'

During one of the times Nigel stayed at our house in Cardiff, my daughter Kathryn was preparing for her driving test theory exam. He was interested in the questions, but out of ten he only knew two! 'It's a bloody good job I ride a bike, most of the time', he said, laughing again.

The only time I really impressed him was when I read to him his poem 'Borders', in Arabic. He used this poem for the introduction to his book, *Real Swansea*:

> What begins for you
> where the waves break
> – sea or land, land or sky –
> depends on where
> you're coming from, depends
> on where you're going to
> and whether you
> have legs or fins, lungs or gills.

He was a huge fan of the H'mm Foundation and helped in establishing its office at Swansea University. He and his folk music group, The Idrisiaid, performed at several varied events. During 2013 for instance in January at Oldwalls Leisure for a debate about Gower, in June at Sketty Hall for an Institute of Directors conference on 'Tourism in Wales', in July in Swansea for an Accountants Conference organised by Bevan and Buckland, and in July at Dylan Thomas Centre for the Institute of Welsh Affairs 25th Anniversary .

His last H'mm commissioned performance was on 17 October 2013 at Morgans Hotel in Swansea, during the Swansea Maritime Festival with Peter Stead. He was as brilliant as ever with his unique voice and style: he read a few poems, the last one being one of my favourite poems called 'Hotel Gwales' and it begins

> There will be, there'll have to be
> a table round as the rings of Sadwrn
> high-back chairs, marble columns and floors
> and two oaken doors as high
> as sky's blue and as sun-fizzing sea.
>
> A cloud for a roof will keep us cool
> and nothing shall we suffer
> of the griefs we've seen

(unless the hand of unwisdom
opens door number three).
Nothing that's illegal
will need to be snorted
for all to be extraordinarily well.

Nigel's only request from me, in all the thirty years I knew him for, was that he wanted to be an 'honorary consultant' of the H'mm Foundation. These are bits of his email to me on 28 October 2011:

Dear Ali,

I have a grovelling favour to ask of you – but only if and when you've time. I have been told by the university to prepare what they call a case study, based largely on myself, for what is known these days as the REF (it used to be the RAE) ... What's new this time round is the interest in Impact ... My colleague Wynn Thomas – who, poor sod, is landed with the job of REF Czar. Anyway, I thought I'd put down the help and advice I have given the H'mm foundation as one example of impact my efforts might have in the wider world... And may I describe myself as an 'honorary consultant' to the foundation?

I haven't had the opportunity to accompany Nigel on his walks, but during the past few years we met in Mumbles, walking on the promenade, taking coffee at Verdi's, not saying much, but still enjoying the walk and company, so that we'd do it again. A word or two about the family, our daughters and plans about going part-time at work. Once we talked about finding a suitable name for the future Welsh Embassies, when the time comes. I suggested the name 'Tongue of the Welsh Inn' and Nigel translated that to 'Tafod Tafarn Cymru'.

It happened ever so fast, and he departed us too early. It was on 16 December 2013 when Angharad called me to say that she couldn't meet for supper in Cardiff, 'Dad was taken to hospital last night, he is seriously ill,' she said with a very upsetting tone in her voice. On 19

December he called me and left a message on the mobile saying 'thank you so much for the flowers, they are amazing … I'm well looked after by everyone here ... must go for a sleep, I have no energy.' On 28 January, Margot emailed to say Nigel had died at the hospice. At his funeral on 10 February, his wicker basket coffin, carried by some of his friends, passed a few yards from where I was standing in the Church while his other friends were singing 'Myfanwy'.

It was only few months before that we were enjoying the taste of 'an oven-baked pheasant wrapped with bacon' – Nigel would email me describing the meal which he was going to cook – he added, 'by the way the bacon is only to keep it moist'.

Publishing a book is always a huge responsibility, and I hope this book will contribute towards promoting and celebrating Nigel's name and his work. I'm delighted with the quality and variety of the contributions. What the contributors have in common is how Nigel's way of life has influenced their own. I'm most grateful to everyone especially to Jon Gower for editing this volume and to Dafydd Prys for putting it together.

Nigel was a dear friend to so many people, among them my own family, my wife Karen and our daughters Lauren and Kathryn.

He was a true friend, an internationalist, a Druid, a limited edition, a one-off.

Introduction – Light Years

Edwina Hart

I wish I could say that Nigel had been my friend but for me he was someone I sometimes glimpsed in events, or was someone I heard when he was reading his poetry, delighted by his ever growing literary respect and recognition.

For me there are many memorable poems. I particularly enjoyed the breadth of his work in *Ambush*. There was a natural pride that a child of Gower had become a poet whose work touched the souls of so many readers. I do not use the word 'soul' lightly: we all identify, I know I do, with music and words that almost become part of your essence. Nigel's poetry had that impact. For me the poem '299792.5 Kilometres A Second' has something very special to say, especially in the final lines...

> Light leaves us as it leaves the stars:
> I see you as you were
> a fraction of a fraction of a second ago,
> sunned at the window, this bitter day,
> by a light that's eight minutes out from home
> we kick heels waiting
>
> And for a sudden upturn, the happy accident
> while gazing perpetually out on the past:
> a quasar as if it was fourteen billion years back;
> a face across the room
> whose light hit the road
> a hundred millionth of a second ago.
>
> think us back some years, you and I...
> Where now, I wonder, is the light of that time?

Edwina Hart is the Welsh Assembly member for the Gower constituency and is the Minster for Business, Enterprise, Technology and Science in the Welsh Government.

Remembering Nigel

John Barnie

— You mean, you've sold my hat — twice!

Nigel Jenkins, Twm Morys, Iwan Llwyd and I were in Bergan Brothers, gents' outfitters, in Syracuse, NY. We were in Syracuse to perform as Y Bechgyn Drwg/The Bad Boys, our bilingual blues and poetry band, but that afternoon we discovered Bergans, a tailor's unlike any in Wales catering mostly, I think, for the black community. There was rack on rack of suits in cerise, kingfisher blue, tangerine and lime green, with jackets available in three lengths, 'lounge', 'matinée' and 'opera', matinée being down to the knees, opera down to the ankles, all in shiny polyester.

As Twm weighed up a canary-yellow suit, matinée length, with matching homburg (he decided in the end that Gwynedd wasn't ready), Nigel paid for a black, broad-brimmed hat, which he put down to browse further among the rainbow colours of the store. While he was doing this, one of the Bergan brothers sold the hat a second time to the 'Bishop of Manhattan', as he informed Nigel with a slightly amused smile when the latter discovered it was missing — the Bishop being an oldish black man I had noticed in the shop earlier, pastor, I suspect, of a store-front church.

— Have you got another one?
— No.

With the help of Mr Bergan, however, Nigel rooted around and found a replacement to his satisfaction, matching it up with a matinée-length black suit, which from then on he wore when performing with Y Bechgyn, and later with Llaeth Mwnci Madoc/Madoc's Moonshine, a trio he and I formed with Iwan. With his imposing physical presence and harmonicas slung round his waist in a specially designed belt, he might have stepped out of a 1940s Western. But Nigel was a fine harmonica player who achieved a rich, sonorous tone in the amplified style of Chicago bluesmen like Walter Horton and James Cotton.

Performing with Y Bechgyn was fun; we enjoyed one another's company, and enjoyed mixing poetry with music which included Twm and Iwan's songs in Welsh as well as blues. There was lots of wine and a certain unpredictability in performance which could be stimulating even if it got us in trouble now and then. (We are probably still *personae non gratae* at Keble College, Oxford.)

The first group Nigel and I formed was The Salubrious Rhythm Co. with Swansea jazz pianist Jen Wilson. That too could be unpredictable. Performing at the 'Wales Week' in Brussels, the PA system was so poor and the hubbub of voices in the pub where we were playing so loud that I couldn't hear my guitar or Jen's piano and kept time by watching her tap her foot. Only Nigel's harmonica reached me, distantly bounced off the far end of the room. The gig was a wash-out and in the end we just stopped.

There were consolations on that trip, though. It was bitterly cold in Brussels and we were not dressed for it. With two days to go before our flight back to Wales, we found a corner pub-café and after wandering around the city in the morning spent our time there, working our way through the bar's list of velvety Belgian monastery beers between ordering lunch and supper. When on our last day Nigel, who spoke French picked up in his grape-harvesting days in southern France, told the landlady we were leaving that afternoon, she gave us lunch for free.

Nigel was not a singer, but his full, rounded bass voice made him a wonderful reader of his own poems. 'Oh I wish someone would bottle your voice!' an admiring woman told him after one performance.

As well as being a bluesman of course he was many other things. For some years he worked as English-language editor of *The Encyclopaedia of Wales* and this added immensely to his already considerable knowledge of Wales and its two cultures. Sometimes, driving with him to a performance, he would invent a character for himself, the nineteenth-century antiquary, 'Cyclopaedic Jenkins', and we would stop off, perhaps at Cilmeri where he would take me over the battle ground where Llywelyn ap Gruffudd lost his life. Another time we stopped at Tryweryn. It was a summer day and butterflies flew around us as we walked across the boulder-strewn retaining wall of the dam. We talked about Capel Celyn and the drowning of a community that brought Mudiad Amddiffyn Cymru into being and galvanised Welsh political life. Looking at the placid surface of the lake, a stranger could not guess any of this, but it seemed cold and alien if you knew. He told me water from the reservoir was released periodically so people could play at white water canoeing in the stream below.

After the *Encyclopaedia* was published he became a member of the English Department at Swansea University teaching creative writing. Perhaps because he knew my views on the creative writing movement this was something we rarely discussed, though when he became director of the MA programme and enmeshed in administration, I enjoyed emails in which he projected another of his fantasy personae, the 'Fat Controller'.

Nigel was a politically committed poet in the tradition of Harri Webb who he admired; he wrote about the drowning of the valley in 'The Ballad of Cwm Tryweryn'. He was not afraid of controversy and must have expected the furore that followed the publication of his flyting on the death of George Thomas, 'An Execrably Tasteless Farewell to Viscount No', when it appeared in *The New Welsh Review*. Walking in downtown Swansea next day, he told me, he was overtaken by a battered car that screeched to a halt. Two tough-looking young men got out and strode toward him. He expected trouble, but they just shook his hand vigorously, got back in the car and drove off.

His poetry also celebrated life in the raw, as in 'Byzantium in Arfon', where a group of American students are exposed to Saturday-night Caernarfon:

> In the Black Boy a jilted bonker
> whines at his mount as she leaves with someone else.
> 'Look,' she shouts back, 'Rwy'n i ffycio fo heno
> a chdi y-ffycyn-fory.'

He always performed this poem with Y Bechgyn Drwg and did so with gusto, certainly for the bawdy, but also because, as the poem goes on to explain, Caernarfon 'is by now the Welshmost town in Wales'. On Saturday nights it might be full of 'the blitzpop blasting from disco-bars,/ the vomit-falls, the can-kicked crowded streets,/ fist, yell, or yowl', but it is a celebration of 'whatever is youthful, loud and Welsh', and that is what counted for Nigel. He embraced all aspects of Welsh life, savoury and otherwise.

He was also a member of Plaid Cymru and a committed republican – you wouldn't find him standing in line at Buckingham Palace to bow before the Queen of England, as some Welsh poets did recently.

As a poet he could be a fine lyricist, an aspect of his work that found expression especially in his two collections of haiku, *Blue* and *O for a gun*:

> at dawn, as at dusk,
> the windows of Swansea
> take fire and burn

Latterly, although he produced the occasional haiku, a form about which he was extremely knowledgeable, the poetry dried up. We discussed this at times. The inspiration had simply gone, and Nigel was too honest a writer to delude himself that it was still there by producing second-rate pastiches 'in the manner of', which it is too easy for poets to do. This was a cause for regret on his part, but he transferred his energies into researching and writing two books for Seren's Real Wales series, *Real Swansea* and its sequel *Real Swansea Two*. These were partly a spin-off from his years working as an editor on *The Encyclopaedia of Wales*, work that developed his love of the peopled landscapes of Wales and honed his eye for telling detail (something equally evident in the haiku). The books were popular. We were in a pub one lunchtime when a man approached Nigel enthusiastically at the bar. I assumed they knew each other, but Nigel had never seen him before. The man had recognised him and wanted to say how much he'd enjoyed *Real Swansea*.

At the time of his death he was working on a third volume in the series, *Real Gower*, and last July he took Helle Michelsen and me on two long walks on the peninsula. To stay with Nigel in his flat in Mumbles was to start the day with one of his legendary breakfasts. All four gas rings on the stove would be blazing, as well as the grill and the oven as he juggled pans with bacon, fried eggs, tomatoes, mushrooms, and laver bread rolled in crushed oats, while toasting bread, warming plates and rustling up cans of strong coffee. Breakfast might be prepared for anything up to four or five guests with a deceptive ease, all the dishes ready for the plate at the same time.

Those were warm sunny days last July and Nigel took us along lanes and down tracks some of which must have been known to few others than himself. His passion for Gower where he was brought up and his intimate knowledge of its layered history meant he was the perfect guide, whether we stopped at Arthur's Stone, the Neolithic burial site on the ridge of Cefn Bryn, or made our way along a path overgrown with gorse and bracken to Vernon Watkins' memorial stone above Hunts Bay. He also knew which pubs had the best beer and several stops were inevitable.

On the second day we were joined by Nigel's partner, Margot Morgan, and descended the cliff path to Bacon Hole. The cave had, he explained, been occupied during the Iron Age, but it must have been as a bolt hole in times of emergency because it would not have been a pleasant place to live. When Nigel shone a torch on the walls it was as if they were covered with a myriad milky pearls — the light refracted from water droplets seeping out of the limestone. Delicate liverworts crowded wet boulders near the entrance; even at the back of the cave where there was a permanent gloom, algae thrived on the dark, wet surface of the rock.

Early on the first evening, Nigel, Helle and I went to Pepper's Wine Bar across the road from his flat. I had been there last with Nigel and Iwan Llwyd when we were rehearsing for a performance as Llaeth Mwnci Madoc and we had sat on the bar's tiny terrace drinking white wine, Iwan's drink of choice. Iwan had died three years earlier, only fifty-two, and we were there now to raise a glass in his memory.

After a long day's walk exploring Gower, we were ready to relax, enjoying the cool wine as Pepper's began to fill with people dropping by on their way home from work. There was that sense of ease and slowness at the end of a summer's day when it seems as though you have all the time in the world. You don't, of course, and as I recall that evening, on the last time we ever met, I remember another of Nigel's haiku:

> how many of the dead,
> as I climb these old stairs,
> do I pass coming down?

Swimming at the Plage Principale

Stevie Davies

When Jon Gower asked me to excavate my diary record of conversations with Nigel, I unearthed a small trove of fragments bearing witness to our exchange. But the journal form is self-regarding – how could it be otherwise? It's a personal scribble, sketching private reflections and observations that otherwise would sift away with the passing moment. The excerpts I've threaded together in what follows, along with quotations from Nigel's poems, our emails and a novel of mine, remember the friend I knew – with all the limitation and eccentricity of such knowledge. You were never intended to read my diary record. For that reason it may offer its own partial but intimate truth. I've made it my rule to alter nothing I transcribe, including ampersands, spelling slips, gaffes, cursory grammar; omissions are signalled in the usual way. The point of such witness is its improvisational quality, the moment-by-moment immediacy of a journal's relation to time. Like Nigel's haiku, the diary form attempts to represent the swift passage of the moment's impressions.

As I leaf through each diary's handwritten pages, I see how oddly it will read to others. For mine is in part the record of an obsessive sea-swimmer. Nigel too was enthralled by sea-swimming. We used to haunt Rotherslade Beach, which he called the 'Plage Principale'. We had both swum with seals:

> The seal's head and mine
> bobbing face to face
> on the tide

And we competed annually to see how long we could keep swimming into October and November. In 2012 I won hands-down:

6 Nov 2012

Yesterday – my last (and it has to be) swim of the year. Excruciatingly cold but I stuck it out for perhaps 25 minutes – & loved it – of course – despite the spent fireworks washing around with the weed (a detail Nigel wants to use in a haiku & I can see why). There was no one there but a guy with a sheepdog which lay so still I thought it was a rock until the rock got up & bounded up the pebbles & steps. So numb I cd not feel to tell if I was wet – laughing away like a madman as I hopped around trying to thread my foot into my jeans. My feet were entirely notional, I cd not feel them even when pedaling home – but felt gloriously scaldingly alive – & feet returned to my ankles when I got under the shower. It was a happy glorious end to our season. Leaves coming down now, yellow, copper, ochre – & ash die-back has not (yet) reached us.

That entry rejoices in the cold sensuality of the element – childlike fun and freedom – the experience of being fully alive in nature. Its most memorable detail strikes me as being Nigel's image-envy: he coveted those 'spent fireworks washing around with the weed'. Sure, I said – have them, they're yours – and looked forward to the poem, but in point of fact I got there first and that curious encounter in space-time found its way into a short story, 'Sea-Path' (2013): 'I decrypt the debris tangled in the rocking drift of seaweed. Cigarette butts, plastic bottles, cylinders of spent fireworks.'

Nigel's haiku would have been so much more immediate and telling than my prosaic list. He'd have alerted our senses, in a handful of words, to that smoky detritus of Bonfire Night ditched among bladderwrack.

> high tide after the storm,
> the bay bobbing with
> bits of forest

> high tide, full moon and
> fighter jets – if their pilots
> could smell this woodsmoke

I was proud to be invoked in *Real Swansea* (2008) as a denizen of the Plage Principale. Nigel memorialised Rotherslade as the haunt of: 'bronzed and grey-haired amphibian "old timers" whose habitual domain – for reading, talking, eating and drinking – is a suntrap in the cove's eastern corner. "I hope we can be like them when we reach their age," Stevie said to me once. I hope so too.' There's a pang in reading that 'I hope so too.' Nigel's family had enjoyed Rotherslade for generations. His uncle, Noel Witts, told me in an email that 'Rotherslade was where my mother lived for many years, so the family came down a lot. Nigel was always part of our annual Swansea visits and gave me a print of Sisley's picture of The Donkey Rock.' Nigel would barbecue for his family on the rocks.

> tide's in, barbie's done
> and 'I can't drink I believed
> the whole bottle

I never knowingly saw – or smelled – the 'barbie'. On 12 September 2005 I emailed Nigel:

Subject: Barbie?
Nigel – that wasn't you making a plume of dark smoke from a barbie on Rotherslade yesterday, was it? I couldn't see over the rocks.
I'm off now for a swim – see you soon. XX
  He replied:
No, we haven't done a barbie for some time at Rotherslade, the girls having been away so much this summer. It would be nice to get one in before Angharad goes to university next Sunday ... I might try and get down to the beach later this evening, after giving the girls their tea. Haven't been in the water for at least a week.

One of my fictional characters, however, saw it all. *Writing The Eyrie* (2007), I needed a beach poet. Waldo is first glimpsed through the scathing eyes and nose of ninety-two year old Red Dora:

But there was a particularly disgraceful figure conducting a barbecue high on the rocks. The stink of charred animal billowed out, interfering with the beach population's legitimate enjoyment. Look at him, there in his cut-off jeans and a cowboy hat, with a reddish beard, waving like a semaphorist who has lost his flags ... Surely the beach would rise up and chase them away?

'Do look at that!' Dora pointed him out to Eirlys.

But Eirlys leapt up and semaphored back, yelling, 'Frying tonight, are we?'

The tolerant beach smiled.

'That's Waldo. My cousin. You've met him. He has the soul of a poet.'

'And how does that manifest itself?'

Eirlys looked puzzled. 'Well, dear, in poetry. And he plays the harmonica lovely, Dora. He can keep it up for hours.'

* * *

Nigel would often talk of the sea and the sensation of boundlessness we experience there, the peaceful, cold 'oceanic feeling', at home in our corner of the world. I frequently noted such conversations – here is one occasion, which led, through Nigel's memorable quotation, on to a landscape of meditation.

6 March 2012

Nigel & I talked about our wonder when we see the stars & sea 'in our moment' – boundless wonder at everything – an atom, a firmament – & he quoted from Pinter: 'Tender the dead' & sent me the quotation. Nigel has the most beautiful mind of anyone's I've ever known – he himself is a source of wonder to me – the firmament within. He helped expose the 3000 year-old Bronze Age causeway in the Bay – which used to be a fen. We spoke about our moment within archaeological time.

Later that day, Nigel sent me this:

Here's the entire quotation, Stevie, from Pinter's play No Man's Land, which Michael Gambon read at his memorial service:

I might even show you my photograph album. You might even see a face in it which might remind you of your own, of what you once were. You might see faces of others, in shadow, or cheeks of others, turning, or jaws, or backs of necks, or eyes, dark under hats, which might remind you of others, whom once you knew, whom you thought long dead, but from whom you will still receive a sidelong glance, if you can face the good ghost. Allow the love of the good ghost ... And so I say to you, tender the dead, as you would yourself be tendered, now, in what you would describe as your life.

Now, in the aftermath of his life, I don't actually think of Nigel as a 'good ghost': he is the most alive dead person I've ever met. This is especially so in the places he made his own – and the chats that were the coda to outings. To share such conversations as these seemed perfectly ordinary at the time: coming and going in our quotidian round, it seemed we had all the time in the world to compare notes. But my jottings show how clearly I recognised the unique preciousness of these exchanges.

Nigel was a great believer in journals and notepads. He was forever reminding Creative Writing students to keep a writer's journal about their persons at all times; to have their eyes and ears open wherever they were; to catch the moment on the wing. In his essay collection, *Footsore on the Frontier* (2001), writing of the haiku form, he insists on the relationship of haiku to the fugitive impressions of the passing moment: 'hardly a day passes without me jotting down in the bum-pocket notebook some phrases towards the expression of a "haiku moment".' Briefly imprisoned in 1988 for his CND action in cutting the wire at the American Naval Facility at Brawdy and refusing to pay his fine, Nigel was allowed to keep his watch, pen and the day's *Guardian* but was denied paper: 'hence this diary kept in shorthand notes in the endpapers and margins of Gwyn Thomas's *Sorrow for thy Sons.*' It was less a desire to fix the passing moment – which for Nigel never could be fixed – than a commitment to record the moment's intimate vibrations as it fled. I think he found in his awareness of transience a strangely consoling thought: all this will pass. Perhaps this relates obscurely to the darker reaches of memory and apprehension.

On 9 June, 2011 I see that I have recorded another conversation, which seems to me to have a tangential connection – though at first sight there's none.

> *Long chat with Nigel yesterday about boarding school. Told him about finding birthday cards I'd written to myself at boarding school in Germany from 'Rose' and 'Lily' – imaginary friends – as I didn't have any real ones – & his eyes brimmed with tears – he was really affected – as others aren't who have never been there. He told me about the Wall.*

The Wall was where Nigel as a child used to go and sit alone when at boarding school, which he loathed. He said it was a good place to cry. But it was also a good place to be oneself. I saw the Wall in my mind's eye as he spoke and knew that I had been there too. We understand of other people only what we are fitted to understand. The eye of each searches out a joint focus. I knew Nigel narrowly but deeply – and only for the last fourteen years of his life. The loneliness of childhood was a place we met. Being sent across the border to an English public school influenced the whole of the rest of Nigel's life: through his rage of rebellion against its values. But the child remained, seated on the Wall.

* * *

By May of each year we were well into the swimming season and we were daily comparing notes about our excursions to the Plage Principale. The next two excerpts evoke the process of reflection we shared.

Fri 10 June
The sea takes us into our little corner of the universe, away
from the social game – we know the universe does not care
for us. It is violent & without heart or direction – but we care
for it. We inhabit, by some marvellous fluke, this nook that
shelters us & where we feel at home & to which we're
adapted – and from here, in our moment, we are privileged
to look out with wonder at this infinity. Told N that I saw
Patrick Moore's 'Stars at Night' yesterday – he was some-
one my parents wd watch – they called him 'Mad Eyes', not
just because of his monocle. Looking into the black mystery
of the beyond – it is absurd to try to fathom any of it – cam-
eras and space machines no more than standing on tiptoe
– & scary too (Pascal's 'Le silence eternal des espaces infi-
nis m'effraie') – but wonderful. This precious drop of being
& contemplation that is my life – these glimpses from my lit-
tle world. Important not to waste time from the
cache of days that will be granted.

Sunday 1 July 2012
Today nobody has bombed us at Mumbles – or broken into
our houses or raped/pillaged/terrorized us. We have lived
under a democracy (just about) & had enough to eat. There
have been no earthquakes, volcanoes or tsunamis in
Swansea Bay because we live tucked into a quiet nook of the
world, unthreatened by the chaos of nature. We've all gone
about our business in this tiny corner without fear – another
day of our very comfortable history – eating nectarines,
swimming in the cold grey sea, reading Sunday papers &
heating up cheese pasties for tea. We have all imagined that
life will go on like this forever – and felt entitled to it. How
astounded we'd feel if a meteorite hit Mumbles – we'd want
someone to complain to. Pompeii was for Ancient Romans.

Within both these excerpts is suspended an awareness of mortality and of the fragility of our peace – and a sense not only that we have not earned such complacent immunity to the planet's hazards but that forfeiture of this privileged 'marvellous fluke' may be demanded. Nigel was pledged, as Socialist, environmentalist and Welsh internationalist to extend the boundaries of wellbeing.

He measured out the contours of Wales by walking his *bro*. His footsteps followed a palimpsest of old tracks, ancient paths trodden by generations of feet. Every moment had a matrix in the long continuum of time. His fascination with 'the 3,000 year old causeway in the Bay' was part of Nigel's obsessive antiquarianism. In writing the two volumes of *Real Swansea* and *Real Gower* (the latter being almost finished at his death), Nigel deep-mapped his and our world. To be with him on one of his expeditions was to be guided by someone who could imaginatively roll back layers of turf, soil and rock, to show you how things had once been.

Ancient churches were his atheistical delight. In my diary I recorded a rainy visit to Neath Abbey in June of 2012. 'Abbey ruins amazing – blown up at Dissolution, great chunks lying sideways where they fell, like the tilted strata of limestone at Rotherslade.' Later the same month:

> *Tues: To Penrice with Nigel, gallivanting in his new old banger. It was lovely – heard Wynn [Thomas]'s talk on Vernon Watkins – he having forgotten his reading glasses & the computer running amok & the church corresponding to Donne's 'Churches are best for prayer that have least light' – but the words luminous ... N & I toured the graveyard via gravestone (illegible, lichened over) of a woman who was murdered – killer's name being apparently scratched out. Had a look in tower, being warned of bats. Never mind bats, it was the gnats that got me...*

> *20 July, 2012*
> *Sunday: tour of mediaeval churches with Nigel in banger – 1st Baptist chapel in Wales at Ilston Cwm, then St Illtyd's Ilston – then St Cadoc's Cheriton – & finally St Llanmadoc*

with the great firs all facing one way in wind, with estuary beyond. Happy time.

Wed 17 July, 2013
Monday – Caerwent & Caerleon with Nigel – picnic – heat – ease & delight in his   company ... we can talk to one another about things that really matter.

In Nigel's seminal essay on Wales, 'The Lie of the Land', he emphasises the impermanence of Wales, quoting the poet Ceiriog: '*aros mae'r mynyddoedd mawr*' (the great mountains abide forever). They don't. The oldest rocks in Snowdonia are young (702 million years old against the Earth's 4,600 million). We 'Sioni-come-lately death-wise bipeds', Nigel goes on, 'have shaped to human purposes and labeled with names ... what it pleases us to call "Cymru" or "Wales". Originating 'far south of the Equator, submerged in shallow, volcano-dotted seas … Wales glided northwards for hundreds of millions of years, a violent passage involving the deaths of oceans and collisions of continents.' His sense of the mystery of global flux and mutation over millions of years elicits all the vigour and hwyl of Nigel's prose. That's one of his styles. The other is pure lyricism. The revelatory haiku (with Tony Conran, he is one of the great Welsh exponents of the form) honour the mystery of the living moment as we breathe it away within that long vista of time:

> but what I see
> > as the jet whines in
> > is the glide
> of a gull
>
> half a dog turd
> bejewelled by a feasting
> blowfly

all paths bombed
by purple bird-splat –
time we picked the blackcurrants

*   *   *

And suddenly we woke to find that Nigel was gone.

against sunned red brick
the pink white explosion
of a lone cherry –

and I don't want to leave it,
the pavement, the day, this tree

Comfort came in pledging myself to swim in Nigel's memory to Snaple Point from Rotherslade for the Pancreatic Cancer Research Fund (www.justgiving.com/Stevie-Davies2). On 11 March, 2014 I wrote:

Tonight I'll eat the last of the blackberries picked & frozen in Nigel's lifetime. Oh my friend, my friend. But it must be done – we have to step away from you, a little every day – and also towards you, in time. Anyway the blackberries – the goodness of the earth, its giving, our gleaning. The goodness of Nigel, his giving, our gleaning.

I swam about 1000 metres today: must build up strength as I've set myself a fearsome challenge for someone not young – & who is afraid, as he was, of swimming out of her depth. But I shall do it. The winter is turning into a beautiful spring-time.

Nigel Jenkins, poetry, his death

Steve Griffiths

An hour before I heard of his death
I saw a kingfisher in black and white
in a fold of January half-light.
It crossed the river away from me.
Wet noise closed in and I lost it:
something rare, keen-eyed
for stillness and every stirring,
welcome in surprised lives,
holding its flash of blue
bowstrung like a good word
for the right unleashing.

Dad

Angharad Jenkins and Branwen Jenkins

A.: How would you describe Dad?

B.: Intelligent. I had a question the other day. It was a grammatical question. I was listening to the radio, and they said something about their debut time at this festival, but they'd been there three times. And I was wondering if you could say 'my third debut time', and I was thinking Dad would have known the answer.

A.: That's wrong. Debut is first time.

B.: Yes. There's been questions since that I've wanted to ask that nobody would know apart from Dad, like little signs I've seen when going for a walk – just numbers. And dad would have known what they were, wouldn't he?

A.: Yes Dad knew everything. Any question about anything – language, history, Wales…

B.: Stars. The first star is Venus, isn't it? I remember Dad teaching me that. What else was he like?

A.: Hairy. That used to embarrass me, when I was really young. If Dad ever picked us up from a friend's house, I was aware that he didn't look like the other dads. He wasn't great at making small talk either.

B.: No. I was always embarrassed because he would just say 'Hello'. Then that would be it, and I'd be thinking 'Oh god…' It was so embarrassing!

A.: Later on, if he used to pick us up from anything, he'd just be sat there. He would have borrowed a car from somewhere, and be sat there hidden by a massive broadsheet, under *The Guardian*.

A.: What do you remember about going to tea at Dad's?

B.: I remember when we used to go after school, we used to try and get up the stairs really really quietly and sneak into the flat, and Dad wouldn't hear us, and then we'd make him jump, which often worked didn't it? But in the winter it was harder because the door would be closed. In the summer the door was always open. We'd usually have something smelly, like curry – really smelly food with lots of garlic in it. He put garlic puree, garlic paste, garlic granules and garlic – all in the same meal! And then tomato puree as well. He loved tomato puree!

A.: Yes. Very flavoursome food. And when Mum used to pick us up, she used to be able to guess what we'd eaten. What was your favourite meal that he cooked?

B.: I liked in the summer we used to have samphire, and he used to panfry some fish in loads of butter. And then I liked his curries. Oh, and his wedgies! He did the best wedgies. I do my wedgies like his now.

A.: How did he do them?

B.: Well, you chop them into wedgies, and then flour and loads of herbs and spices, cumin, and seeds – I can't remember the name.

A.: Was it the ones that he used to put in curries?

B.: No, not the 'flavour bombs'. And chilli and turmeric, and he'd mix it all up and sprinkle it on, and then toss them up. They were lush. And I quite liked his steaks as well. When we used to have salad, steak and wedgies in the summer, that was nice. And he'd always have some beer in the fridge.

A.: Always booze...

B.: Booze, olives, and nice bread.

A.: Olives from Carwyn's.

B.: And stinky cheese. Urgh...

A.: Do you remember he said he'd put the cheese on the back seat of the car...

B.: in a plastic bag, to make it sweat. Oh, that's so disgusting! I remember once – you know he used to keep it in the Tupperware box where the glasses are. I opened it, thinking I quite fancied a slice of cheese, and there were white things crawling on it!

A.: Cheese mites. Do you know in France, that's a good thing.

B.: I know. And Dad was like 'Oh yummy. Cheese mites.'

A.: It's something that people ask for.

B.: That's so disgusting!

A.: Tell me about the time when you went to Gower of the hills, north Gower.

B.: We went there, and we first stopped near where they're building some power plant. And there was this house on a hill, and he was saying that the government employed this bloke – they called him Deathray Matthews – to invent a death ray to ray all the Germans. And he'd done some inventing. He'd projected pictures onto clouds. He was a bit of a wacky inventor. When he was practising this death ray, all he managed to do was stun a few cows. He's got what looks like a crazy man's shack on the side of a hill. And then we left there and carried on going on this really straight road. And then stopped in the place where Dad had been before. And there were all the bullets from when the Americans were practising. It was like a firing range basically. But firing at each other. And the big military people... you could see where they'd put their guns, because there were humps every now and again. And there were little tiny trenches where the men would be lying, and they'd have to duck. And there were just thousands of old bullets. So me and dad went round picking some of the best bullets.

A.: How would he say the story to you about Deathray Matthews? Was he excited about it?

B.: Yes. Sometimes it would be really boring though. But because he knew so much, he would have to pick and choose what he said to me, because I only wanted to know about the interesting stuff, the crazy stuff.

A.: Tell me more about him on that day.

B.: When we parked in the first place, he had a really old pair of binoculars, and he was saying that his binoculars were really clumpy. So I bought him some new binoculars the Christmas before last.

A.: What else do you remember about that day?

B.: He had a wee. I remember that.

A.: Where did he have a wee?

B.: By Deathray Matthews' house!

A.: Dad used to love the way you say 'beef'.

B.: I don't think I used to say it like that.

A.: A little bit. It was quite cute, when you were younger.

B.: Getting less cute with age...

A.: What about when he was dying? How was he then?

B.: He'd have nice times, like when he was in the bed, and you and me were on both sides, and the curtains were drawn, and he said 'I can see peas and chips'. And we were saying 'Does it look nice?' And he said 'No. Not particularly.' And he knew he was just seeing stuff, but it was quite nice to make a conversation about it, and not make it weird. And then we said, 'Are they mushy peas or normal peas?' And they were mushy, weren't they?

A.: I can't remember.

B.: And then he said he saw Dylan Thomas down towards the left-hand side of the bed. And he said he could see faces. And we said 'Are they nice faces?' And he said 'Oh yes, very nice'.

A.: And we said 'Are they friendly faces?' And he said 'Yes' And we said 'Do you recognise any of them?'

B.: And he said, 'No, not really. But Dylan Thomas is down there.' And then I think the same time, we started singing 'Lucy in the Sky with Diamonds' and that was really nice, because he wasn't in pain, and he wasn't worried. That was nice. Do you remember on the Monday morning, he was stroking my face. And then I wanted him to stroke your face. So we swapped places for him to be able to stroke your face, but he turned back round, and started stroking mine. And before that, he wanted me to help him on the commode...

A.: He trusted you a lot more, being a nurse...

B.: He was very open. He didn't hide anything. We could ask him whatever question we wanted.

A.: Like?

B. Have you had a good life? Have you got any tips? Are you scared?

A.: And how would he answer those questions?

B.: Just very honestly. He said he's not scared of dying. He's just scared of the pain. And then you said to him, 'You've had a good life, haven't you?' and he said 'Yes, very good'. And you asked 'Have you got any tips for life?' And he said, 'Go for it'.

A.: He directed me to Epicurus. He's a philosopher who basically said not to fear death. And then there was a poem as well. I've written that down in my diary.

B.: He says when life stops, death stops too. He said he found that quite comforting, didn't he?

A.: Yes.

B.: I think we did as well because it... I remember a few days before he died, just wanting him to die, because he wanted to die.

A.: I think that was a help for us, in a way. He didn't want to be there any more.

A.: Was your relationship with Dad different to mine?

B.: Yes. I would say very different. You would go to literary stuff together, and then I would be the one who would go on nice walks with him. I think it was last summer, he took me to this cave that's by Pennard.

A.: Did you go to the cave?

B.: Yes.

A.: I've been to the cave.

B.: And there was a bat. The time before when Dad went there, there were loads of bats. And I've never seen a bat before. And Dad took me, and there was this bat there, and Dad was trying to make the bat fly at me, by being noisy. He knew that I didn't want lots of history and stuff like that. But these places did have bits of history. There was this graffiti in the cave from early nineteen-whatevers. And then we'd go for nice meals out. It would usually be the Langland Braz. It was more days out and going for walks, whereas with you it would be the literary things.

A.: Did Dad talk about literary things with you?

B.: Not really.

A.: Why?

B.: Well, it's not that I'm not bothered. It's just not my forte. I'd just like to go to pretty places and go for a coffee. I'd like to talk about horses, shopping and weddings. And Dad liked horses.

A.: You were riding for a while, weren't you? Did you have conversations with Dad about horses?

B.: Yes. I used to ask Dad's advice. I remember there was one time I had a really lazy horse, and Dad was giving me tips about how to keep it in canter. And then about three summers ago, we went horse riding together across Gower. We went to Parc-le-breos. I'm not a good horse rider at all. At this point I hadn't even had any lessons, so all I could do was trot. And we stopped off at the King Arthur, and had lunch and a pint or whatever, and then went back. And there were some people didn't have a clue how to ride. And there was Dad and another lady. And even for me these horses were rubbish. It was an effort to get it to trot. And Dad was getting a bit bored. The other lady asked to have a canter, so she and Dad and the instructor held back, so they could canter up to us. And when Dad came up to us, he said, 'Oh I think my horse struggled a little bit with me'. The horse was making really painful noises. And then we were talking about the best stuff to feed a horse to make it nice and agile. But Dad liked twitchy horses, ones that would just go. And I'd just want a fat cob who just plods along! Do you remember the story that Dad would tell us about when he was younger, and he took one of their horses out, a twitchy one. He went for a ride, and he was galloping back to the stables. He was getting closer, and thinking to start slowing the horse down a bit. They were really close to the stable door, and the horse was still going. And dad jumped off the horse, and the horse just ran straight into the stable door.

A.: Is that why Dad had a scar on his chin?

B.: Yes.

A.: Do you know Corinne's got a scar and Tom's got a scar? And possibly Martyn and Carey as well. All on their chins – from horse riding.

B.: I remember when we first went horse riding to Clyne, those hats that had the bit over your chin. I always wondered why they were there. Maybe that's why they're there – to stop everyone who rides horses having matching scars. They've just got straps now. I think that was quite a dated thing, having the bit on your chin. I enjoyed talking to Dad about horses in the last four years or so. We didn't really have much in common, but we both liked the horses.

A.: So you've been riding more recently, but he used to take us to Clyne every Saturday. He was a farm boy at heart.

B.: Yes. Definitely.

A.: Being out on the horse probably gives you time to think, doesn't it? But he did like being on his own. I remember asking him, 'Why can't you live with anyone?' and he said 'Because I'm absolutely rubbish before 11 o'clock. I can't talk to anyone before I've had a cup of coffee and read the papers. I just can't be with anyone.'

B.: That's funny. I don't remember, when we used to stay over, him being really grumpy.

A.: No, but those times were special, those weekends. I think he could probably do it once a week, but not all the time. But I remember having a conversation with him about relationships, because I worry that I'm like him. I worry that I'm never going to be able to live with anyone. I think I was probably in the middle of breaking up with Jo at the time. I think I was asking him for advice. I used to like talking to Dad about relationships.

B.: I don't think Dad was the best person for relationship advice. He was a serial playboy!

A.: He said he liked being on his own.

B.: Not too on his own though.

A.: No. But I think he like having the freedom.

B.: Yes.

A.: The flat on his own.

B. Yes. Yes. No pets. Nothing. Banished. His flat was lovely, wasn't it. Especially when he got the new sofa. And there was his armchair. And the left side of the armchair is more worn than the right, because the fire was next to it. I've hardly ever sat in that chair, because Dad would always be sat in it, wouldn't he? So we'd always be on the sofa or the rocking chair.

A.: Do you remember playing hide and seek in the flat, in the dark?

B.: Oh yes! I loved hide and seek in the dark.

A.: Do you remember I hid just in the shadow. I was in the middle of the room. You and Dad couldn't find me anywhere. But I wasn't hidden behind anything. I was just sat in our bedroom.

B.: Oh yes, in the corner, where that chair is now.

A.: You couldn't find me anywhere. But then you and Dad made me laugh. And I started laughing. And Dad was saying, 'Oh oh I can hear something'.

B.: We used to play that hide and seek in the dark a lot, for a while. And Mancala.

A.: Do you remember you used to get really annoyed because Dad used to pronounce words of things in their proper accents of the language, like Ratatouille and Barthelona.

A.: Do you remember when we used to get the bus back home to Caswell – there was a bus driver who was obsessed with Dylan Thomas. And he used to quiz Dad, 'Nigel, do you remember the name of Dylan Thomas's dog?' – knowing that Dad was a poet and a writer. But I don't think Dad knew all those things. Do you remember what Dad used to say about Dylan Thomas in the Uplands? When Dylan Thomas was a little boy, he stole his aunty Eluned's purse in the Uplands.

B.: Yes. He took me for a walk – last summer I think. It was quite a long walk. We went from Caswell across to Brandy Cove, and then Pwll Du, and then across a little bit further. It was a walk that he took some people on in the Gower Walking festival. I think he was blagging it a little bit. We got lost a few times. And we had to back-track quite a few times. And there was one bit, he was saying all these stones are little grave stones, because there was a boat that had prisoners on it. And the boat hit some rocks. And I think the sailors and captain just got off and left the prisoners to drown. And near Pwll Du, there's lots of little stones in a circle. He also said we were related to Barti Ddu.

A.: He's written a poem, 'The Ballad of Pwll Du Head', about the prisoners that were drowned. Yes, we're related to Barti Ddu. I think his aunty used to say that. And we're related to Jemima Nicholas.

B.: I was going to say Jemima Puddleduck!!!

A.: Don't you remember going to Jemima Nicholas's grave? She's the woman who dressed in red and walked around the headland to scare the French off – the French were coming to invade Britain.

B.: It's just a typical Jenkins type person – an absolute nut case!

A.: Yes. Jemima Nicholas is related to us, but I don't know how or why. These are questions I wish I'd written down.

B.: These are the type of things that Dad is the only person who would know, who could give us a clear answer. So now I think it's just lost. We're never going to know. I just don't know how he knew so much.

A.: He had an incredible memory. And it was all to hand. Everything was there.

B.: Yes. It wasn't 'Oh I've got a book. I'll just check.' He'd know it straight away. That's what I can't understand – how can anybody know so much? About everything. Not just literary stuff. Beers. Wines. Plants.

A.: The body.

B.: Birds. Stars.

A.: Geology.

B.: *Daearyddiaeth*.

A.: Rocks.

B.: That is geology.

B.: What's *daearyddiaeth* in *Saesneg*?

A.: Geography.

A.: The history of Wales. Do you remember going on tours of Wales with Dad?

B.: When we went to Shell Island? And Dad introduced us to the ice-cream in Aberaeron, didn't he?

A.: Honey ice-cream. Didn't we go on a couple of tours of Wales? And we'd stop off at various places. It was like a guided tour. He'd pick out places of great cultural and historical interest. Like the pylon in Aberystwyth that was something to do with S4C.

B.: It's so funny. Because it's not what an eleven-year-old wants to do. I think then we didn't really appreciate his knowledge, not until the last five of six years.

A.: And we got a train from Porthmadog to Blaenau Ffestiniog. And we just wandered round Blaenau Ffestiniog for the afternoon! Getting really weird looks. Do you remember that? And he took us to Tim Davies, the artist. He's got an old converted chapel. He knew about everything.

There'd be books everywhere. And his flat had a very distinctive smell.

B.: Garlic. And wine.

A.: And fires.

B.: Yes.

A.: And slightly dusty.

B.: But tidy.

A.: Very tidy. I think the dust was a firey dust.

B.: Not a dirty dust.

A.: And he loved chocolate.

B.: There was always a half-open bar of Lindt. And if there wasn't, he'd send us to Castle News to get another one.

A.: He used to like Toblerone as well. Tobla. He used to shorten words quite a lot. Barbie instead of barbeque. Rothers instead of Rotherslade. Tobla instead of Toblerone.

B.: I remember going to his flat after the raft race with Carys. And he said, 'What have you been drinking?' Just asking. Not giving us a row. And we said rosé. And he said, 'Oh, pinko plonko'.

A.: Ah! Pinko plonko! He used to do massive feasts. I remember one time I was meant to have a friend come and stay for the weekend, and she didn't turn up. And Dad had bought an absolute feast of food. And he was really annoyed because he thought all this was going to go to waste. So suddenly I had to invite all my friends over to eat this food. And it just so happened that none of my girl friends were around that weekend so all these boys came – Matthew and Dafydd and Owain and Owen Bidder and Christian Richards and Matthew Evans – all the boys. And there was a huge feast. And Dad was just so generous with the food and wine. It would just be flowing.

B.: He loved entertaining.

A.: Yes. He lived quite a simple life really. He had this tiny little flat with no central heating.

B.: No car until the last few years.

A.: No holidays. But I think he used to spend his money on...

B.: ...champagne, olives and cheese.

A.: Fine wines. Mumbles Fine Wines. Didn't he have a membership at Mumbles Fine Wines?

B.: Yes. Dad loved the Anjou didn't he? That was his ultimate favourite red wine. And then they stopped doing it in Mumbles Fine Wines. And he contacted the vineyard, and asked them to send him hundreds of bottles, but they didn't reply. And he would go back to Mumbles Fine Wines, and ask if there was anything else. And I went recently, and I said I was Nigel Jenkins's daughter, and I was saying about the Anjou. And they were saying, 'Oh yes, he did love that one didn't he? He said he was looking for something – the closest we could get to that. I showed another Anjou to your dad. So he bought a bottle, and he came back, and he said, "Mmm, keep on trying".' He knew what he liked and didn't like. Mmm, keep on trying.

A.: I remember he came to stay with me in uni. In the first year, and as part of my performance module I had to go to lots of different concerts and review them. So I got us two tickets to the Sheldonian theatre to see a classical concert. There was an orchestra playing Debussy. This theatre is famous for being really really uncomfortable. The seats are in an amphi-theatre kind of shape. And we were sat there, but the seats are so close your knees dig into the people in front of you. It was all very respectable. And then after, because Dad had spent some time in Oxford, he knew about lots of places which, at that point, I didn't know because I was in my first semester. And he took me just round the corner from the Shelodonian to the Turf Tavern. It's one of Oxford's oldest pubs. It's as if Oxford has been built round the Turf Tavern. You go down this tiny little alley way, and stumble on this really old olde worlde English pub with fine fine ales. I wasn't an ale drinker then but he bought me a pint of Abbot, which is quite strong. It was really really nice. It was really full as well, so we had this little seat just by the door. We were just perching there really. There was enough room for two of us. And he bought me another. And another. And another. And I think we'd had about five pints of Abbot which is a lot. I had such a lovely time. Dad was recalling the days when he was working in Leamington as a journalist, he came to stay with a friend of his in Oxford who I think was lecturing there, and how they also sat in the Turf Tavern drinking lots of ale. And his friend had dared him to drink a pint of ale out of his boot. So Dad said that in the Turf Tavern, about forty years ago, a young Nigel Jenkins would have been there supping ale from his boot. But I remember coming back, and being really quite pissed, and my house mates were down in the flat downstairs, and I introduced my dad to everyone, and Dad was just being cool, and quite funny. He was saying something like 'Yeh, these are my dead father's boots' or something. I just remember him being really random. I've forgotten loads of things, but Joe Allen said that one day, because I wasn't very good at keeping in touch when I was in uni, Dad left a message on my phone going, 'This is God calling. Just wondering if you're alive.' But I think as we got older, that was when Dad really enjoyed our company, because we were more like adults then, and we could join in – we'd appreciate his intellect and his information more. And we'd enjoy a drink. So it was more like an adult relationship. And I bought tickets to go and see John Cale with Dad. He was a big fan of John Cale. Do you remember, he used to pick me up from uni in the van. And crossing the bridge, we sang 'Take a look at my girlfriend, she's the only one I got, durra durra durra, she's not much of a girlfriend, I never seem to get a lot.' Dad loved that song. When we used to cross the bridge back into Wales, it became a tradition to sing it.

B.: I still sing that when I come over the bridge now. I turn the radio off, and I sing it.

A.: Ah, Dad loved it because it was Supertramp – I think it was a sample from Supertramp.

B.: That was how it came about. We had the radio on and this song came on, and we couldn't work out how Dad knew this song.

A.: But that used to happen all the time. Dad always knew in modern pop songs when things were sampled from when he was younger. And he'd also have an ear for things. I remember listening to S Club 7, and they sampled a really well-known classical piece. He had such a good ear. We used to listen to Keith Jarrett and Cyndi Lauper and the Beach Boys. And he'd love songs like 'Time After Time', the bass line.

B.: Yes. He always loved the bass line.

A.: But he'd pick out unusual things, 'God only knows what I'd be without you'. That was one of his favourite songs. And he loved Miles Davis.

B.: Do you remember that jazz trio CD that he had. It was winter, and it was a Saturday night, and we were staying at Dad's. I was probably about fifteen or sixteen. There was the table with the light on, and we'd had our food, and we'd had some wine. And Dad had probably given me a bit too much wine for my age. I remember the blues CD was on. I started singing along to it, and I was saying, 'Oh my god, I now know why you all love blues so much'.

The Key to All Our Houses

Noel Witts

Nigel: poet, essayist, historian, editor, teacher, performer, ironist, walker, drinker, cyclist, swimmer, harmonica-man, cook, beach-barbecue-man every year with us at Horton. He was also my cousin, the person with whom I could talk, and my major contact with a country that I had left for what, in those days, we thought were better things in England. Most of my life has been spent in English universities, so that my twice yearly visit to Swansea would mean a catch up with Nigel's career and family. We would, inevitably, talk about the politics of Wales, the crass state of UK politics, the bureaucratic boredom of academia, and sometimes, but not often, his own writing – he left that for me to discover. For me he was not only my bi-annual confidant, but a constantly surprising flower from an Anglo-Welsh family which had no literary history.

'Born on a farm in Gower' says the accepted blurb, but we know he was actually born in Gorseinon Hospital! However he definitely grew up on the farm on the Kilvrough estate a few hundred yards from where he is buried – the church at Pennard – and where he spent much of his 'unspent' years growing.

I happen to remember when he was born. Gloria and Rowland – his landowning father and his industry-linked mother – decided that I should become 'Uncle Noel' – a heavy responsibility at the age of eleven, which was only relinquished when it became a bit too embarrassing for us both to sustain. At that time we lived in Sketty, and it was always a treat to come down to Kilvrough for the day to see how this young family were all getting on...

The house where Nigel grew up was a wonderful old farmhouse with a yard full of secret outhouses, and a marvellous room called the Saddle Room, which Nigel often recalled – full of horse tack, bridles and saddles, and smelling of polish and animals. Nigel and Martyn and Carey, his brother and sister, were all great riders, and they must have known every wall and gate and path and field all around the farm. A few years back Nigel took my daughter Romilly riding at Rhossilli, and I remember then being amazed that such a by-now-grand literary personage could look so at home in the saddle! Years of training, of course...

In his wonderful book on Gower, with photographs by his friend David Pearl, he lists the names of the farm's fields, where he lived and grew up – names such as Cocklebushes, The Lawn, Six Acres, Stallion Paddock, Deer Park, and the field next to Pennard church, which was Church Park; and then there was Poppins Park, which led to his great grandfather's cottage just down the road from the church.

But then, like many Anglo-Welsh families, it was decided that he should go away to school to be educated. The institution of choice was Dean Close School in Cheltenham, to which I and his father Rowland had also been sent. I had quite a good time there, but Nigel hated it and referred to it as 'that totalitarian dump'. He was, in retrospect, probably correct. Martyn, his brother, tells a wonderful story about Nigel pinching the battery from the school bus to put in his old Austin, recently acquired for a fiver, and hidden at a friend's hotel. The acid leaked from the battery and ruined the school uniform: meanwhile the school was in turmoil because its bus, for some reason, would not start!

Then came the work as a reporter in Leamington Spa, from which he learned the skill of asking the right questions, and there were the travelling years – Europe, North Africa, a circus in the USA, and of course India and the Khasis. There was the time at the University of Excess, as Essex University was known in those days, where he began immersing himself in Wales and the Welsh, before returning in 1976 to live in a Nissen hut on the farmland with his wife Delyth. They moved to Mumbles in the '80s, where his two daughters, Angharad and Branwen were born, and where they were sent to a Welsh school. He was trying to get rid of the Anglo...

The rest you all know – the writing, the broadcasting, the India book *Gwalia in Khasia*, the essays, the editing of the massive Welsh Encyclopaedia – known as the Psycho – and the research for what I think are the two masterpieces of psycho-geography – *Real Swansea 1* and *Real Swansea 2*. It's important to reflect that although he was referred to in most of the obituaries as a major poet, it was his prose work that often, in my view, exceeded the verse. It brings to mind the work of Dylan Thomas, who could write a broadcast piece as well as a poem and who also was a lover of a drink or two.

Nigel didn't write much about death, nor did we ever talk about it, but there is a wonderful passage in a piece he wrote for John Peel's *Home Truths* on BBC Radio 4 in 2000, in which he says the following:

> *The ancient Celts believed that no one truly died : you simply shuffled off into the Celtic underworld, and could return from time to time to mingle with the living. And that's how it seems in our dreams sometimes, when the dead come back and wander round inside our heads, insisting by sheer force of presence, and the persuasiveness of a conman, that surely there's been some absurd mistake, they never died, how could anyone have imagined such a thing? ... But with an after life in the memories of the living, the dead rarely leave us alone for long, and as far as most of mine are concerned, they've got a key to the house and can wander back in whenever they want.*

I think Nigel now possesses the key to all our houses.

As we got older our conversation inevitably turned to discussing our ailments, the number of pills we had to take, and equally inevitably how to stop drinking. My image of Nigel's conversation was of him seated in a large chair with an equally large pint beside him, while we would both pontificate on the state of the world, the state of our families, and the state of our glasses. But an equal memory is of his wonderful cooking in that kitchen in Mumbles and his inevitable hunt for fresh sewin for us to eat with some well-researched wine.

Nigel's response to the medics was typical. It's all there in 'Teetotalitarian Lament', which starts:

Pour oh pour that booze away
Said my conscience when it came to call
And spotted the dozen bottles of hooch
I had laid up in the hall.

And so on.

Two weeks before he died I read him an article in *The Independent* by Boyd Tonkin, on climate change and Gower. I was, of course, somewhat apprehensive about what he would think of the opinions of such an interloper. But he said 'Good, it's not at all patronising' and, I thought, it is largely due to writers like you that it is getting less possible to be patronising about Wales.

On my next visit to him at the Tŷ Olwen hospice, when he was really weak, I read him a short story by one of my favourite writers, George Mackay Brown, the Orkney writer who hardly moved much from his home in Kirkwall, and as I was reading it I realised that Nigel was a kind of Welsh equivalent – a writer whose home locale is his major inspiration – the Swansea and Gower chronicler for our times.

On my last visit to his flat in Mumbles, I asked him about the old maidenhair plant, which was still in a pot on the table in the window. He said he should really split it each year but had not done so this year for whatever reason. There was a real sense of him winding down, though not so much that he could still give us directions to see the extraordinary gravestone of St Cennydd at Llangennith Church at the end of his beloved Gower.

He may have gone, but in some ways we are lucky; we have his words, and that is indeed a privilege.

My favourite of all his writings is probably his poem 'Maidenhair', which unites his love of his family, his interest in nature, and his unerring ability to find an image which says so much more than its words. Here we have the old great grandfather, his grand mother, and the plant looking on. This is something that only poetry can do, and the reason why, of all the many things that Nigel could do, I think that writing was the best.

MAIDENHAIR

The fern was all I wanted there;
The richer pickings – her lustre jugs,
the family dresser – were spoil I left
for other tastes. Grandpa's fern,
that dwelt with her, dwells now
with me, a mist of light
on the dark shelf.

Have I the touch, the
whispered skills, to bring it
after so hatred a season
to its old brilliance?

I breathe fern, and say ancient
link with primal trees
and the forests of heat locked up
in coal. I say grandpa's fern

and she who taught me
the naming of this and many things
opens a door
to rooms of sunlight and polish and fruit.
There sometimes we've found him, clouded
in smoke, a froth of ale beading
on his walrus moustache,
as he fumes against
progress, the workers and his gout.

They are dead, and their story.
There were things
I'd meant to ask: when to cut back?
what if, say, something –
a bullet perhaps – were to smash

its jar…how then to
re-pot – with leafmould or peat?

The maidenhair endures in the Celtic west.
Theirs they kept whole lifetimes
in the same narrow pot.
I'll give it space, learn its ways; help it
flourish, reproduce, watch me go.

Then, of course, there's the other ribald Nigel, which was a major
part of his ironic character:

TEETOTALITARIAN LAMENT

"Pour, oh pour that booze away,"
Said my conscience when it came to call
And spotted the dozen bottles of hooch
I had laid up in the hall.

So I pulled the cork from bottle one
And poured it down the sink –
Apart from just one glass of the stuff,
A little farewell drink.

Then I pulled the cork from bottle two
And did more or less the same
Except this time I drank two small glasses,
For which thirst must take the blame.

From bottle three, three glasses I took,
From four, yes, four I drank.
Then I grabbed hold of both the bottles
And poured 'em down the sank.

I pulled out the cork from sink number five,

Poured the bottle down the glass and drank it,
I then pulled the sink from the cork of the next,
Bottled seven whole pours and sank it.

From the next full sink I pulled the glass
And bottled the cork down the pour,
I pulled the cork from my throat, the glass from the pull,
And drank a few sinks more.

When I had emptied everything
I steadied the house with one hand.
And counted with the other the bottles and corks –
Some fifty at first I counted.

I counted again when the houses came by,
And got 'em all, about a hundred, I think –
All except for one house and a bottle
Which I promptly proceeded to drink.

Returning to Cefn Gornoeth

Deborah Llewelyn

> She who has forgotten
> remembers as if yesterday
> the scythe they left rusting
> in the arms of an apple,
> the final bang of the door
> on those sheep-bitten hills.
>
> In Abertawe, in Swansea
> there were killings to be made,
> and they politely made theirs.[1]

Mid-morning, June 2012, and the sun's already burning the back of our necks. Nigel and I stand before a long, low gravestone in St Cadog's churchyard, Llangadog, reading the inscription:

> *In memory of Mary Anne, daughter of David and Anne James, of Cefengornoth in this parish, who died May 6th 1805, aged 8 years.*

These are Nigel's ancestors, the James family, from whom his paternal grandmother, Dilys, descended.

'I know so little about them,' says Nigel. 'The family lived at Cefn Gornoeth farm for generations, until my great grandfather, William, left in around 1910, to seek his fortune in Swansea. My grandmother was born and grew up at the farm, but when I asked her about her childhood, she always claimed she'd forgotten about it.'

We leave the churchyard and cross the humpback bridge, joining the footpath that follows the left bank of the River Bran and leads up to the farm. Nigel has brought me, one of his MA students, on this expedition as I know the country well, having grown up a couple of miles down the road and played at Cefn Gornoeth as a child. The village of Llangadog is at our backs now, humming with traffic and gossip like a summer beehive. My spaniel Flora prances ahead, pausing to look back, checking we're following. This is a well-established route for her, one her nose and eyes know well, but it's all new to Nigel. He's curious about everything: the path, which shows no sign of human footfall, and resembles a grassy lawn; the ornate kissing gate we pass through; the woodpecker drumming from a dead oak, completely hollow, which he climbs inside to catch a glimpse of the bird.

We follow the river's winding course through pasture starred with celandines and daisies. Thrushes call to each other and pheasants croak from the wooded hill. The river is clear and fast flowing, overhung with willows and alders, dark and deep under the farther bank. 'Plenty of brown trout in here I should think,' says Nigel, 'and sewin swimming upstream in the autumn.' I tell him his family would have had fishing rights here as the river runs through their land. He admires the rich red earth of the riverbank. 'What's the bedrock here, Debs? I'm never totally happy in a place till I know what rock is under my feet.'

'Sandstone and mudstone. Millions of years ago, this area was a deep sea bed.' It's unimaginable; and yet this river, the Bran, and the Ydw and Tywi and the Sawdde are all running in search of the sea; they feel its pull, and in straining towards it they've carved this valley into its gentle fluent shapes. This is a country of streams and rivers branching into one another, the land between them rising and falling.

We pass into fields where ewes are grazing with their lambs, crows sauntering among them. We're treading an ancient footpath which has seen centuries of use, which Nigel's ancestors would have used as a shortcut into the village, or to herd their animals to market.

'My great grandfather, William James, ran the mart in Llangadog, then in Llandeilo,' says Nigel. 'He farmed here and was also an auctioneer. There used to be a picture of him on the wall of BJP Estate Agents in Rhosmaen Street.'

'What did he look like?'

'Quite stern, a determined set to his jaw. William set up an office in Swansea, and he ran the cattle market on Tuesdays on the green outside the King Arthur hotel in Reynoldston and at the Commercial Inn at Gowerton.'

'So how come you're not Nigel James?'

'William's daughter Dilys married Tom Jenkins, my grandfather, a Gower lad. Tom was a land agent at Kilvrough, Gower, he bought the two farms when the estate was disbanded.' He tells me how the fortunes of his forebears rose after marrying into a family of wealthy Swansea industrialists. Yet something was lost; as they developed a taste for servants and public schools, they forgot the Welsh language and culture.

> She spent a lifetime loving
> the taste of white bread, a lifetime
> forgetting the loser's brown.
> And on their middle floors
> the brass gleamed, the crystal sang,
> while away in the attic
> dust fingered
> the violins and the harp,
> and far below stairs a discreet
> and calloused tongue complained.
>
> Years she remembers
> of cuff-link and shoeshine,
> but nothing, she says, nothing
> of those dung-filled yards.[2]

The footpath leaves the riverbank and leads us up through steep sloping fields, along the edge of a hanging oak wood. Looking out over the countryside as we climb, we get a sense of the whole of it, the undulating fields, the small farms folded into the hills, the wooded slopes. We climb past ash trees full of untidy nests; crows caw at us as we pass. The warm air smells sweetly of bracken. Nigel admires the dense blackthorn hedges which he is glad to see have not been grubbed out as so many were when the European Union gave grants to farmers to create huge fields. 'So much history in a hedgerow. You can tell how old they are by counting the plant species. And so rich in wildlife.' He finds a jay's feather, striped turquoise, black and white, and sticks it into the rim of his cowboy hat.

Nearing the top of the hill we can see far out over the countryside to the south; the radiant pastures, emerald and lime green, the wooded notches of the streams, the tawny Mynydd Du, Mynydd Myddfai and beyond them the scarps of Llyn y Fan. I point out Y Garn Goch in the south west, the hill topped with an Iron Age hill fort which Nigel has written about at length. 'As I get older my obsession with history and prehistory is growing,' he says. 'There's so much we can only guess at, that's downright mysterious, like Y Garn Goch. Who built it? It could have been the Celtic Demetae tribe, or the Silures, or some earlier civilisation, we don't know. Why is it called the red cairn? Is it because of the bracken turning red in the autumn, or folk memory of some gory battle that took place there? They left us so few clues.'

As we press on uphill the top of a Wellingtonia breaks the horizon ahead. We catch a glimpse of a long driveway, mature oaks and beeches, and an imposing farmhouse at the top of the rise. 'Those trees would have been planted as part of the landscaping of Cefn Gornoeth in my family's time,' says Nigel, 'probably in the late eighteenth century.'

We follow a quiet grassy track through the old orchard, only a few gnarled apple trees left, wisps of wool on the bark where sheep have scratched their itches. 'The farm has changed a lot in the last ten years,' I tell Nigel. 'It's not as I remember it from childhood, there's been a lot of development in the last few years. It's not a working farm anymore.' The grey slate roof of the farmhouse shows above the hedgerow, and we're through the final gate and into the yard.

I haven't prepared Nigel for this sight; his face betrays the shock. This isn't the ancestral farm he was expecting to see, but a conglomeration of luxury barn conversions. I try to explain. 'After the last owner died, it fell into the hands of property developers. They knew how to work the planning system and got permission for six extra dwellings.' Nigel stares around sadly. The place is deserted; it's a weekday and everyone's out at work. My spaniel sniffs around disconsolately. Where once were cobblestones and the wholesome whiff of cow manure, there's now a dung-free concrete parking area. Where chickens strutted and chased each other, there are neat front lawns with picket fences.

'It's the same old story,' says Nigel. 'Same thing happened at our farm at Kilvrough. It's so hard to make a living as a farmer these days. As your income gets less and less, debts mount up and the land gets sold off piece by piece. The younger generation don't want to farm anymore, they can have a better standard of living elsewhere. I didn't much fancy putting in twelve hour days, seven days a week, for a pittance, either.' He wanders over to a huge stone building that is now partitioned into executive dream-homes. 'What did this use to be?'

'It was the old *sgubor*, a barn with stalls for the heavy horses they used to work the land. In the war, Italian prisoners of war were stationed here, they slept in the *dwlog*, up there, the hay loft. Jack Evans, who was the farmer here then, used to ring a bell from the farmhouse at six oclock every morning and they all filed down and washed in a stone trough that used to be over there, where that BMW is. Those holes in the top of the gables were for doves. There used to be nesting boxes for them inside.'

'That's the trouble when this sort of thing happens,' says Nigel. 'You lose all the history, all the culture of a place.'

We wander over to the farmhouse, now a listed building, the back part being the original, oldest part, the front a nineteenth-century addition. There's a cellar with a stream running through it, I tell him; it's haunted by the ghost of an old farmer.

'Could be one of our lot,' he says, smiling at last.

Other ghosts have left their traces; the remains of the old *twrchdy*, where once I scratched the long, dusty backs of pigs, is a tangle of collapsed bricks, nettles and corrugated iron; the clogged pond, once the domain of ducks and fierce, hissing geese is now home only to water weed; and the woman, Dilys, who remembered 'nothing, nothing of these dung-filled yards' is now, herself, only a memory.

At the eastern end stands a long, low building which catches Nigel's attention: a typical Carmarthenshire single-storey Welsh longhouse. It's in the midst of being renovated; the left hand side is roofless, the back wall collapsed. It was built five centuries ago from stones dug from the fields and carted from the river Sawdde. We step carefully through the gaping hole which was once a doorway.

'This part is the *beudy*, where the animals would have been kept', says Nigel. There are still rusted hitching rings mortared into the walls inside, and an old lintel for the door which would have led through to the living quarters, two rooms, living room and a kitchen, and a *croglofft* in the roof, reached by a ladder.

'I remember this being used as a dairy, when I was little, then as a stable', I tell him. 'It was the original farmhouse, much older than the big one.'

Nigel is pleased to hear that the couple who are renovating this house are taking their time over it and using local materials. He runs his hands over the smooth stones of the walls. 'Old red sandstone, from the river. Look how rounded they are, like big pebbles.'

We follow the lane past what used to be the bull pen, lambing barn, chicken shed and milking parlour, all now 'desirable residences'.

'I remember watching the cows coming home up this lane from the fields to be milked,' I say, 'swaying and spattering as they went.'

'Same as at our farm in Gower,' says Nigel. 'My grandfather named all his pedigree friesians after women in the family. There was a Molly, after my grandmother, Gloria, after my mother, Dilys, Eira, Eluned, Gwyneth, Alice, Wynne, Helen… and the bull was Hector, named after himself!' He tells me that his maternal grandfather, Captain Hector Leighton Davies, spent most of his working life as a director in the steel and tinplate industry. Farming was a sideline in later life, to be approached with technological precision, and 'all mod cons.'

Continuing down the track we pass what used to be the kitchen garden, now a jungly wilderness of weeds, and come to a gate with a sign, 'Gornoeth Stud, Welsh Cobs'. Further up on the hillside five black cob mares are grazing. Nigel leans over the gate and calls 'gup, gup, gup!' They raise their heads, prick their ears and come trotting down to us, manes and tails floating in the breeze. They vie for Nigel's attention, arching their necks, their noses soft as moles.

He's ridden ponies and horses from before he could walk, Nigel tells me. One of his early memories was re-enacting the chariot racing scene from *Ben Hur* with his brother, their steady old 'bomb proof' Welsh mountain pony, Fairy, pulling them in an old pram tied to her bridle with two lengths of baler twine.

His father, Rowland, had a passion for hunters, and on Sundays the family would ride out, his mother beautifully dressed and riding side saddle, never astride, his father on his big glossy hunter, Mascot, followed by Martyn, Carey and Nigel on their ponies, trotting down to the beach at Three Cliffs Bay, or Pwlldhu, or up along Cefn Bryn.

'We were so lucky,' Nigel says. He has so many memories: of getting up as the first streaks of dawn were in the sky and riding his pony, Bayberry, down to Pobbles beach, to gallop through the Pill at Pennard; cantering bareback into the sea in the summer, wearing only cutoff jeans, letting the big horse, Kismet, swim; galloping through the waves, the sun spangling through the spray as it flew up around him; being mistaken as a girl in horse shows because he'd braided his long hippy hair into a plait.

'These are beautiful cobs,' he declares. 'If anything could tempt me into becoming a horseman again, it would be one of these.' They breathe over him their grassy breath as if in blessing.

1: 'Yr Iaith,' Nigel Jenkins, *Acts of Union*.
2: 'Yr Iaith,' Nigel Jenkins, *Acts of Union*.

Nigel Jenkins (1949-2014)

Robert Minhinnick

Early this year (2014) I attended a lecture and film describing plans to construct a 'tidal barrage' in Swansea Bay. The film began with predictably magnificent marine vistas. And then the commentary began.

'That's Nigel', I said. As did my wife. Nigel Jenkins's rich baritone was unmistakeable. The best reading voice to come out of south Wales since Richard Burton.

'He's not well', I added.

Then, three weeks later…

That Nigel was lending his talents to support an innovative renewable energy scheme was typical of the man. In the past he had also opposed the spread of opencast mining and the construction of on-shore wind turbines. There was no dichotomy in this stance. He wanted the landscape, its history and cultures, protected. Opencasting, he felt, destroyed too much. Wind turbines, especially in historic areas, were pointless intrusions.

Always I found Nigel a man of firm beliefs. He loathed bureaucracy wherever he encountered it. He knew it wasted time and resources. He also railed against 'pedagogy', attacking those writers and teachers he labelled 'peds'. I imagine many who read his articles about 'pedagogues' would have wondered 'does he mean me?' I did.

This could be amusing, but sometimes Nigel was wrong – as he was about Cary Archard, the creator of Seren Books, publisher of Nigel's poetry collection, *Song and Dance* (1981), and much later, his prose works *Real Swansea One* (2008) and *'Real Swansea Two* (2012). In truth, Nigel owed Cary the debt that all writers owe their editors. Frankly, editors cannot win. But Nigel seemed to object to Cary Archard because he was a schoolteacher. A mistaken antipathy.

When Nigel Jenkins died he had himself become a respected Director of the Creative Writing programme at UC Swansea. He was hardly a ped, but his position was an irony many might have anticipated.

One of my favourites of his books is *John Tripp*, published in 1989 in the Writers of Wales series by UWP. Here is Jenkins getting his teeth into a congenial subject, producing a knowledgeable but not uncritical appraisal. (No hagiographer he). I recall the three of us in the Old Arcade, next door to Cardiff Market. Nigel was forced to act as mediator as myself and Tripp stood up to one another over Tripp's use of the phrase, 'twittering optimist'. Good humoured but sternly authoritative, Nigel kept us apart. Soon afterwards we three repaired to the fabled 'Alfresco Club' (a bench in The Hayes) where we could peruse 'the tragic cabaret' (another Trippian phrase) over a flagon. It's hard to credit now that John Tripp was only fifty-nine when he died, and Nigel sixty-four.

Noting the readability of the monograph on Tripp, it's our misfortune that Nigel was not commissioned to write the assessment of Harri Webb, when the latter died in 1994. Webb, in some ways, served as a role model for Nigel. In their middle years both poets felt poetic inspiration and energy fail. But Nigel pushed himself to become a mordant balladeer and satirist. (Thus he is one of the few poets to be published on the front page of *The Guardian*, with his swipe at House of Commons Speaker, George Thomas. (Talk about an easy target.)

Yet, unsurprisingly for a trained journalist and driven writer, Nigel discovered he was able to describe successfully the parts of Wales he loved and understood. His work on *Gower* (Gomer, 2009) and *Real Swansea* reinvigorated him. I believe at his death he was at work on *Real Gower*. Whereas Webb's silence lengthened, reflecting his cultural alienation.

Nigel's championing of Tripp, Webb and later Tony Conran, exemplifies this need to honour and to discover a role model. (Nigel edited *Thirteen Ways of Looking at Tony Conran* [Welsh Union of Writers,1995]), and his energy for organising events and literary celebrations until the end seemed boundless.

A major part of his life was thinking about the Welsh language and attempting to become proficient. He became a regular collaborator with Menna Elfyn, translating her poetry, and co-editing bilingual anthologies for Wales Anti-Apartheid Glas Nos, (CND Cymru) 1987 and other groups.

Recently he mourned the death of Iwan Llwyd (2010), with whom he had collaborated (alongside John Barnie and Twm Morys). Indeed, public performance was a major part of his artistic impulsion. He played mouth-harp in a poetry and blues band, and I'm sure there were exciting plans for the future, especially as his partner, Margot Morgan, is a noted singer, and his daughters, Angharad and Branwen, musicians.

Recommended reading now is surely *Footsore on the Frontier* (Gomer, 2001), an excellent prose collection. This includes the depiction of John Tripp's wake, 'It was what he would have wanted', and 'Diary of Prisoner WX 0674', written by Nigel in Swansea gaol, in 1988, for refusal to pay a fine after a CND demonstration. Also collected there is 'The Tradition that Might Be: The Folk Poets of English-Speaking Wales', which remembers Cyril Gwynn of Gower. Nigel was no folk-poet, although he learned from the tradition. Nigel's championing of Gwynn and others was part of his awareness of the value of history, as real as his opposition to open casting, on-shore wind turbines and literary bureaucracy. Some readers felt him too kind to these English-writing 'beirdd gwlad'.

However, whenever the bureaucracy he hated ignored writers he valued, he could be scathing. But his own plans for a restructured literary organisation in Wales failed to win official support. I think, if realised, his scheme would have been thrillingly radical. But it also would have exhausted him in endless attrition.

Nigel, in fact, was embroiled in arguments with Swansea council and residents about his own 'street poetry' in the run up to the 'Year Of Literature' in 1995, and the creation of Tŷ Llen, its major venue, now the Dylan Thomas Centre. This was all part of his instinctive democracy and love of fair play. In a way, Nigel was too idealistic, too decent a human being to be involved in the internecine conflicts of professional literature.

As to his poems, I recommend *Acts of Union: Selected Poems 1974-1989* (Gomer), and 'Ambush' (1998). This latter indicated the way Nigel's poetry would develop, into the haiku and senryu of his later volumes. The former's 'Never Forget Your Welsh' is both biting and ambitious. His most ambitious prose is found in *Gwalia in Khasia*

(Gomer, 1995) which became Wales Book of the Year, leading to several television programmes. But I prefer essays such as 'The Lie of the Land' (collected in *Footsore on the Frontier*), his depictions of Gower, and always 'the magnetic field of Swansea'.

Nigel's writings are too broad for easy categorisation, but I would expect Gwasg Gomer to work on a generous critical perspective to the poems, when the present shock of Nigel Jenkins' death has been absorbed.

Bard of Gower

Peter Finch

We were in a long room above a pub somewhere in Neath. My family had once been in the beer trade around here selling ale to thirsty bargees and workmen covered in dust. This fact could have made me a local but it didn't feel anything like that. Nigel was teaching a creative writing class and I was the brought-in help.

The creative writing movement was one of the things that Nigel really believed in. Encouraging others to write, getting poets to improve their craft. He had a laid back approach, gain good work by example, expand the students' reading horizons, be there when they floundered, offer constant support. He was everything the traditions around us were not: sceptical of authority, open to the new, an advocate of the alternative, a practitioner of poetry as literary entertainment, a true believer. 'Those bastards wouldn't recognise real poetry if it came up behind them and attempted to bugger them on the spot,' as once said Bryn Griffiths, or something similar. Nigel felt the same.

These were creative writing as a taught activity's early days. Classes were funded by the trade union-supported Workers' Educational Association. A people's activity. Almost everyone in attendance at Neath was unemployed. At the time Nigel's politics were roughly where the border is between communism and anarchy. He owned the Pelican edition of the Marx/Engels *Communist Manifesto* and claimed a certain fluency. He encouraged me to write to Chairman Mao and asked him if he had a poem he could contribute to my journal, *Second Aeon*. I'd done this putting 'Chairman Mao, Peking, China' on the envelope, but the great man had not replied.

Socialism was important to Nigel. He disliked privilege and the authority that came with it. In the early post-war decades the communist way was still seen as the answer, something I could never quite get my head around. Nigel had suggested that I read Santiago Carrillo's *Eurocommunism and the State* which would explain everything. The text was impenetrably dense. Thirty years later I reminded Nigel that he'd once offered this wonder to me as an easy to get into explanation of the way ahead. 'Might not have been the best of my suggestions', he admitted. I gave my copy to Oxfam last year, still mostly unread.

But these were the south Wales late 1970s and there were edges out there to be pushed. I'd been invited to Neath as a prominent member of the Anglo-Welsh avant garde, a sound poet, a guest at the class, there to explain just what sound-text poetry was. Encouraged by Nigel I'd done a run of sonic recreations of Kurt Schwitters, Ernst Jandl and Bob Cobbing, hardly household names in Wales, and then finished with a blast of my own stuff. I could roar with the best of them. Sound poetry, as Henri Chopin had discovered, worked best when you exposed language's micro-particles. In the dusty room, clustered as we were around heavy metal-legged tables and with half empty glasses before us, I explained a little of what Chopin had meant. This involved me imitating the Frenchman's tape recordings of his own body sounds and adding vibrato by banging my chest.

At the back someone evinced the opinion that this was all, actually, crap. A common perception. This was not what Pound meant. T.S. Eliot would be spinning in his grave if he knew. Dylan Thomas would be aghast. This didn't, however, prevent one of Nigel's more enlightened students from vocally disagreeing. Lively debate was encouraged here.

It's not crap, the second student complained, it's good. No it isn't, was the immediate reply. The two squared off. You just don't know what poetry is, one of them shouted. I bloody do, replied the other. There was a big scraping of chairs, a sort of scuffle, and then fists began to fly. God this poetry is exciting stuff, Nigel told me, as he leapt forward to separate the fighting pair. And it was too. With Nigel at the heart.

Throughout the rest of his long career Nigel kept himself there. At the heart. Whatever else he became famous for – and there were a great many things – he still called himself a poet. First and foremost. For Nigel poetry flowed in the blood. Even during the years when he was immersed in relentless ten-hour days working on the *Encyclopaedia* he still regarded verse as his main and most important job.

Although never much of an experimenter himself, not quite, he supported those who were. And if there was an underdog out there, someone not getting the right treatment, someone neglected or grossly misunderstood then Nigel would be the man to champion their cause. He supported the work of tri-lingual Welsh-Canadian extreme concretist Childe Roland, for example.

He was instrumental in getting Roland's *YOUUUUUUUUUUU* piece installed in a wall just behind Morgan's Hotel in Pier Street, Swansea and then getting the poet down to the Dylan Thomas Centre to perform his work. He then backed the successful bid to get Roland offered full membership of the Welsh Academy. When Dave Hughes came up with his first and, at the time, much derided Swansea dialect poems Nigel was at the front, supporting him. He believed strongly in the Welsh tradition of the Bardd Gwlad, the folk poet. Welsh writing in English, he claimed, was an 'utterly arse-about-front literature' with a full range of talented practitioners, publishers and critics but hardly any readers. We needed more poets who had the people's ear such as Harri Webb and the writer Cyril Gwynn from Gower. He cited Irene Thomas of Ebbw Vale, artist, ballroom dance teacher, spiritual healer and poet with a feel for her people and their history, as a fine example. As others emerged Nigel gave them his support.

The mainstream was not where he felt most at home and despite his not inconsiderable success out there at the top of the tree – the BBC, The Arts Council, the posher publishers of Wales – he never lost touch with the other way of carrying on. Idris Davies, Webb, Gwenallt, John Tripp, Mayakovsky, Brecht, Cardenal, Ginsberg, these were his heroes. He was a prominent member of that thorn in the side of officialdom, the Welsh Union of Writers. 'That it exists is vital,' he told me. 'It doesn't necessarily have to do anything. The fact that it is there is enough.'

In America they loved the sound he made when he spoke. I was with him in upstate New York where he was fronting his poetry and music group Y Bechgyn Drwg. Dressed in Stetson, long black coat and cowboy boots he could have doubled for Johnny Cash. Harmonicas in a row were attached to his belt. A foot-tapping, blues-chanting Welsh Captain Beefheart. But it was the Richard Burton-like sonority of his voice that engaged his audience.

In the nineties the Arts Council of Wales took the decision to divest itself of most of its literary services and seek an independent provider. Divestment was in vogue, move the state one further step back. The Council invited bids. I joined what became the successful contender based around the Welsh Academy. Nigel and Dave Woolley were each involved with credible rival operations. After what seemed to be an age officialdom finally made its decision in the Academy's favour. Some rival bidders were unhappy with the process and there remained, for a time, a certain amount of tension. On a personal level none of this leaked over into friendships I had established with both Dave and with Nigel.

In 1998 the Academi had also won an unprecedentedly large lottery grant for the production of an *Encyclopaedia of Wales*. This project had the historian John Davies at its head, academic Menna Baines as Welsh editor and Nigel Jenkins to handle the English edition. In terms of Nigel's literary career this new post represented a significant shift away from creative anarchism to academic precision. He took on the work with relish.

As with many grand designs there were overruns. The hopelessly optimistic notion that two years would be enough proved false almost immediately. Time spun out like chewing gum. A series of funding supplements were sought to keep the show on the road. These were hard to obtain and increasingly so as successive new deadlines collapsed under the weight of their own improbability. In the end the project took a decade to complete, one which Nigel bore with equanimity. He'd signed up for twenty-four months. Bearable, just. And now here he was with his life seemingly lost forever deep under the matter of Wales.

At the project's height, with the editors saying that, yes, it would only take another two years and the funders declaring that enough was enough, the idea emerged that, to save money, the books should appear as they were. This would mean publishing them unchecked, at least to the academic standards demanded by the publishing press (UWP), and with English and Welsh editions significantly unco-ordinated. The editors were aghast. Such a proposal would present Wales as a Micky Mouse nation. The only alternative was for those involved to agree to finish their work within six months, the extent of existing financial resource. At a meeting high up in the skies at the Academi offices in Mount Stuart Square tables were banged and strong words were exchanged but agreement was reached. The editorial team would deliver. We can do it, they declared unanimously, and everyone shook hands.

It was at this point that Nigel's computer caught a virus. This particular piece of malicious tomfoolery attacked the machine's data files, randomly selecting pieces of text and mailing these out to contacts listed in the users address book. The virus went to town. It took large slabs of internal correspondence between the three editors and banged these out to the world. My inbox began to fill up with messages from Nigel that consisted of slices from his correspondence with John and Menna. Very John Cage. But there were things being said here that it was best that the world did not know. I rang Nigel to tell him that his team's approach to officialdom was being laid bare. There was indrawn breath. 'What shall I do?' 'Run the virus checker.' 'Do I have one?' 'See that McAfee icon?' 'Yes.' 'Give it a press'. Nothing more was said.

Nigel's completed script was delivered in 2006 with the Welsh files arriving a year later. The books appeared to great acclaim in 2008. Nigel bore the scars of wrestling with what he called Psycho right up to his death. Creating the books taught him more about Wales than he'd ever known possible but it also compromised his ability to make other creative work for a considerable stretch of time.

In the latter part of his life, post-Encyclopaedia, the haiku, that three line form, seemed to take the place of his earlier longer verse work. His twenty-minute cycle ride from Mumbles into the University where he co-directed Creative Writing with the novelist Stevie Davies was just about long enough to come up with seventeen new syllables. He told me once, walking across Swansea Bay in early 2012, that he thought poetry might, at long last, have deserted him. 'I just haven't written much in recent years,' he confessed.

'Does that mean you can no longer hack it,' I asked?

'Certainly not' was the immediate reply.

We'd worked on psychogeography together. His take on Wales's second city, *Real Swansea*, had been a great success. He'd followed it with *Real Swansea Two*, was fervently arguing for a volume three. 'There's so much material', he kept telling me. Before he died he had also virtually completed *Real Gower*. Gower was his heartland, the place he was born in and the land he knew the best. He'd convinced me that making it Real, as it were, could be his most successful creative act. He'd even suggested that he was going to buy a car to help him get round. 'Can't do it on my bike, boy. Too many hills.'

Nigel had taken me around Mumbles as research for my then forthcoming Seren title, *Edging the Estuary*. Mumbles was where he lived, where he bought his fish and fresh veg, chatted to neighbours and took the air. Not quite Gower but no longer Swansea either. We did the oyster beds, the castle, the yacht club outside which Kingsley Amis had stood, cigarette in hand, the remains of the tram terminus, the restored Ferro-concrete apple café on the headland, the Mixon sand bar made famous by Edward Thomas. He was keen also to show me the Bronze-age ancient track way that archaeologists had discovered leading out into the waters of Swansea Bay. We headed out to sea, walking.

'What are we looking for,' I asked?

'Wooden slats, fossils, laid out like a path. They could have been lifted, but I doubt it. They are here somewhere.' We turned in many circles, spent thirty-minutes on the sea line, fruitlessly kicking at sand clumps and mounds of pebbles. Salt water up to our knees. Found nothing. And that non-finding, as Nigel later pointed out, was in itself a perfect psycho-geographic act.

In the Tripp days, which we'd both enthusiastically shared, much of the journey would have been punctuated by drink. No pub could have been passed without entering and the problem of stop tap would have been solved by hip flask and bottle in brown paper bag. I was never a member, however, of the famous Cardiff Hayes Island alfresco afternoon drinking club. Nigel and others of similar bent would attend this between the end of Welsh Academy Executive Committee meetings and official pub opening at 5.30 pm. 'You wouldn't be there, gwboi', as Nigel pointed out to me, 'because you'd have been diligently manning the till at Oriel.' Members included Tripp, Robert Minhinnick, the late R.S. (Bob) Thomas, and several 'thirsty winos who'd run out of booze and knew a good club when they saw it'. Fellow Academicians, such as chairman G.O. Jones, would shuffle embarrassedly by the club with a shy wave.

In the USA I witnessed Nigel exiting an upstate liquor store pushing the American equivalent of a Tesco trolley, full to the top with bottles of wine.

'I think I might be an alcoholic,' he confessed.

'Have you lost weekends,' I asked?

'Not really,' was the reply. Indeed, unlike other drinker-poets, Nigel was never seen falling off the stage nor lying down across the front of the urinals. I could not keep up with him. Constitutions are different. At his funeral there was champagne drunk at the graveside. Nigel had insisted. What sort? Extremely good. His daughters threw glassfuls onto the coffin. 'For you, dad.' Sustenance for the trip on to the next world.

It'll be hard now not having Nigel out there on the other end of the phone and always ready to respond to emails. Like me he was a hater of Christmas and in the early days did almost everything he could to be in work away from it all while the festivities rumbled at home. For many years we'd celebrate this fact by phoning each other to commiserate while the rest of the world was eating turkey.

He looked outwards, always wanting to know what was going on. He was one of the few in Wales who'd followed the London poetry wars of the seventies and was familiar with how verse was everywhere from Serbia to San Francisco. He also understood and valued the little magazine and the small press. He ran one himself, *The Swansea Poetry Workshop*, publishing unknowns and setting them against the prevailing mainstream tide. He knew who Wales's champions were, the real ones. He possessed one of those rare Hemingway devices, a built-in, shock-proof, shit detector. He knew who our chancers were. He tolerated them with ill-ease.

He valued our country and hated to see it maligned, misrepresented or misunderstood. He was patriot to the core.

Others better qualified than I can write about his place as a traveller, peace protestor, editor, critic, essayist, prize-winner, associate professor, linguist, administrator, walker, harmonica player, *bon viveur*, broadcaster and donkey jacket wearer. The jacket, that one with the embroidered shoulders. He must have worn it for forty years.

Nigel, we'll miss you. But because of the writer you were you won't vanish. Jenkins, Bard of Gower. You'll carry on.

Farewell, Fellow Editor

John Davies

I first came to admire Nigel when I read the type-script of his *Gwalia in Khasia*. Who else, I wondered, can write such splendid prose? Here is his comment on flying above Bangladesh: 'Pincered between the lethal surges of the Bay of Bengal and the annual deluge of monsoon water, much of it draining off the Khasi Hills, these coastal Bangladeshis are seasoned precisians of life's murderous whimsicality.' And these were his feelings on meeting the couple who looked after the cemetery in which Thomas Jones (The Founding Father of Khasi Alphabets and Literature, as his gravestone describes him) is buried: 'All that separated these two survivors from the lethal poverty of Calcutta's homeless thousands was this ramshackle boneyard and a Welshman's grave.'

I was hugely proud that my commendation was printed on the cover of *Gwalia in Khasia*. I took the book with me when I visited Shillong. A waiter informed me that the book was being serialised in the local English-medium newspaper. I went to see the editor, who informed me that 'your archdruid is in town'. I visited the Polo Towers Hotel and had breakfast there with Dafydd Rowlands, T. James Jones and Tegwyn Jones. It was Nigel Jenkins, therefore, that led me to meet the head of Gorsedd y Beirdd not far from the borders of Tibet.

I was delighted to hear that Nigel, with Menna Baines, would be joining me as editors of *The Encyclopaedia of Wales*. (We were fortunate that Peredur Lynch also became part of the team.) Our task was to prepare two volumes each containing nearly a million words, work which took far longer than the two years originally allotted to it. During those years and during the additional ones, I am happy to confirm that, among all the editors, there was fruitful co-operation and friendship.

I was amazed at Nigel's capacity for hard work, and his skill in turning the turgid writings of some of our contributors into translucent sentences. Meeting him was always a delight; his superb deep voice created a wondrous sonority and his conversation was constantly amusing and imaginative. When working on the *Encyclopaedia*, we would send each other at least half a dozen e-mails a day, but I have hardly met him since the work's publication. Recently, I thought of going to Swansea to see him, but then came the dreadful news of his serious illness. To realise that I will never see him again is the cause of the deepest sadness.

Marwnad, o fath

Menna Elfyn

Who now will gather snowdrops?

'Can
        a flower?
Can
        a poem?'

Seeds blown,
will they be welcomed,
these native tremblers

will they give new breath
to the burial ground,
whisper to the living

of a man in a coat,
hunter of flowers.
Will they? Will you

see their light?
'I know what I am
doing here',

said the bard,
bardd gwlad,
who asked only

for snowdrops,
'a warmer world',
hallowed ground.

* *

Byddem yn dadlau
am ddirgelion yr *haiku*.
Mynnais ei bod yn ddull

We'd argue,
haiku's mystery;
to me, too succinct

ry gwta heb gyfleu
ehangder delwedd.
Heddiw, yr amheuwr

not allowing the vastness
of an image.
today, an agnostic,

sy'n deall cryndod,
tair llinell o unigrwydd,
a'r gweld yn gafael.

I understand the shiver
three lines of loneliness:
to see- is to hold

Glas-nos:
nosweithiau glas
glesni'r bore

Blue night:
blue grass evenings,
morning, eyes of blue

* *

'*Hope I can deliver* Real Gower *on time'* –
note at beginning of December 2013

You were 'Real Gower',
the druid of oak,
its strangeness – your *cynefin*.
every talar, scope for a story.
You laughed , repeating your childrens's charge:
'*dim hanes*', no history the little ones said
when you took them hiking.

Today, I know all those histories
poured like the living stream,
will satisfy their hearts with tales
drawn up, forever new.

But not today. No, not today.
First we must turn to the history
of grief.

**

Buried in the boots
you bought in Asheville.
I was there; bore witness
as you chose, discussing
the relative merits of various pairs,
some too tight,
others just right, leather softer,
more yielding.

And for fifteen years
the boots were a source of teasing.
After all there was much
of the sheriff cowboy about you,
the kind of man who, when he hit town
would be mobbed by the crowd,
eager to be within earshot of that powerful voice,
laying down the law, just and measured.

Only one thing missing—
your steps, as a cowboy
were never that heavy;
your learning
was worn lightly.

Nothing wild about you,
And as for a gun?
You were the empty handed
peacemaker with nothing
but your boyish pocket knife.

And I bid you farewell,
not in a wicker coffin
but on your stallion
as you make your way
into the wilderness,
sunset ablazing,
I daresay you'll rest awhile
in some stream by the mountain.

**

*Too many funerals
of friends* we sighed
as we arrived
at Conran's departure.

Driving back south,
your hand at the wheel
and a barn owl flits
as it lit our lane homewards,
an ember in the sky,
beating its warmth,
eager for life.

Duende, I said then,
Conran's soul
leaving the land.

Today, that owl
is in my heart
hauntingly present.
And you, *cyfaill*, *Cymro*,
incomparable *compañero*

no longer the driver.
Let the road ahead
be steady.

Handholding
(*following a visit at Tŷ Olwen Hospice, Morriston*)

I'd ask you to hold my hand
tightly as the plane rose,
the fear of oblivion
within me. Rising-
to its zenith?
Thermodynamics : so hard to understand.

Today, now I know
you cannot rise above
the turbulence of clouds –
so hard to comprehend.
Far from the touch of my hand,
I could not even return
one final favour.

And yet, I left you
among your loved ones,
keeping vigil,
their hands upon you
to ease your flight.

Nothing for me to do
but drive homewards,
through motorway's overflow,
to the wailing of wipers,
the tyres screeching.

**

Dyma'r mis y byddet yn mynd
i chwilio am eirlysiau,
lawr yn y meysydd a'r gelltydd,
eu byseddu'n dyner,
gweld y byd trwy glychau iâ
eu glendid.

Heddiw, addefaf yr af
yn y dirgel ryw ddydd
a phlannu eirlysiau
yng nghladdfa'r gymuned,
fel y byddi'n blodeuo
bob blwyddyn, a dof
ar eu trywydd i'w gweld
yn siglo, a chrynu
yn atseinio i'r plwyf
dy enw.

**

February, your month
to search out snowdrops
down in the fields and woods,
touching them tenderly,
seeing the world through their
ice-bell purity.

This day I vow I will
some day, secretly
plant snowdrops in the
common burial ground,
you then
will flower each year, I
will follow their trail to watch them
swaying, shivering,
ringing your
name
throughout the parish.

Notes

Cynefin: a Welsh word for place (of belonging).

Talar: acre.

Bardd gwlad: poet of a particular area.

Claddfa'r gymuned: Pennard Community Burial Ground.

Glas-Nos: title of anthology we co-edited for CND Cymru in the eighties.

Asheville: a place in North Carolina we visited together as part of a month long tour of the US as ' Three poets from Wales'. The third poet was the late Iwan Llwyd.

Conran: At the end of January 2013 we travelled to Tony Conran's funeral in Bangor and on the way back, a barn owl narrowly avoided the windscreen.

Common burial ground: Pennard Burial Ground and a reference to the fact that his wish to be buried there was refused by Pennard Community Council.

Would You Like a Fork?

Delyth Jenkins

It was a few days before Christmas in 1977. Some mutual friends, the crew from Open Cast Theatre, were holding a party in the Vivian Hall in Blackpill, a rather insignificant looking building on a stretch of coast between Mumbles and Swansea. In true seventies style, there were candles in Mateus Rose bottles, and the Bull's Blood was flowing.

Our hosts had laid on a good spread – quiches, plates of ham, and many different salads such as green salad, rice salad, pasta salad, coleslaw. The plates were stacked up, ready for everyone to help themselves. But there was one crucial omission – they had forgotten to bring cutlery. Somehow or other I had managed to procure a fork from somewhere, so I could eat the coleslaw and rice salad without any loss of dignity.

And then I spotted him. He was wearing jeans and a white shirt. Most men in the seventies had long hair, but his was really long. Black and curly, contrasting with the white of his shirt. And there were the John Lennon glasses. He was swigging from a flagon of Brains, and contemplating the buffet with bemusement – how to tackle all this without cutlery. My possession of probably the only item of cutlery in the room was an ideal way of approaching him.

'Would you like a fork?' I asked.

In future years, when people would ask us how we met, he would recount my words to him at our first meeting, and then add his inner unspoken response: 'Blimey, we've got a posh one here!' And then he would throw his head back and guffaw in his inimitable way. He recounted this tale time after time, and never failed to laugh mischievously at his own joke.

We spent the rest of the evening together. Neither of us were particularly good dancers, but I seem to remember we were up on our feet dancing all evening. I was wearing a long Laura Ashley skirt, which must have had a good swishing movement! And as we danced, we talked and talked. Nigel told me that he had recently returned to Wales after working as a journalist in the Midlands, and then travelling round Europe and America before going to university in Essex. And he mentioned quite shyly that he was beginning to write poetry. He also mentioned that he was learning Welsh, and he was very keen to try out his fairly basic skills on my Welsh, which at that stage was not up to much either. And we went on to discuss other things beyond our own personal history. As we were at a party being hosted by a theatre company, the discussion turned to the subject of entertainment. We discussed at length as to whether entertainment had any value as purely entertainment, or did it have to have a more serious purpose. I remember we were poles apart on our attitude to Noel Coward! The discussion that evening was a foretaste of the relationship that was to come. As well as the romantic and physical attraction, there was a meeting of minds. In the years to come, we would spend countless hours discussing all sorts of things – theatre, poetry and literature, art, travel, religion, politics in general, but especially the politics of Wales, which he was returning to with all the fervour of a convert. These discussions would usually take place in our favourite drinking holes – the Joiners in Bishopston, and in Mumbles the Vic, the White Rose when it still had a cosy little snug with an open fire, and the Pier which also had an open fire.

As the party in Blackpill drew to a close, it was time to say goodnight. Nigel offered me a lift home, but as I was sharing a house with one of the hosts of the party, I thought it might look a bit forward if I accepted his offer, especially as his way home was in the other direction. We didn't kiss that night, but we exchanged phone numbers. I think we both knew then that we would be together very soon. There seemed to be no doubt that this was the beginning of a long and significant relationship. It was the first and the only time in my life that I have felt like that.

So we went our separate ways, he to spend Christmas with members of his family in Parkmill, and me off to my parents in All Stretton in Shropshire. During that time we didn't contact each other, and I never mentioned to anyone my encounter with a mysterious tall, dark and handsome poet-in-the-making in a scout hut in Blackpill.

Way before the days of mobile phones, Nigel seemed to sense that I was back in Swansea, and the phone rang almost as soon as I had got back. We arranged to meet up immediately. Our first date was in the Vic in Mumbles, which in later years after we moved to Mumbles was to become our local, and was the location for many a wild lock-in.

From our first meeting and our first date, we both knew, as surely as the sun rises and sets each day, that this relationship was going to be significant and long-lasting. We did not discuss how this exciting new love affair might develop, in the same way that we did not discuss if the sun would rise the next day on a new dawn.

And so I became a frequent visitor at his Nissen hut in Kilvrough, and he to my loft room in a house that I shared in Brynmill in Swansea.

The year that I met Nigel, I was doing a PGCE at Swansea University. I had done a degree in English and French, and although I knew that I did not want to be a school teacher, it was in the days of grants, and so doing a PGCE put off the day when I would have to decide what I was going to do with the rest of my life. Towards the end of the year, I still had no clear idea of what I wanted to do, and by this time the Protestant work ethic had kicked in. I had to do something to justify my existence on this planet. So I started looking for all sorts of jobs, including teaching ones. I applied for a post teaching French and Drama in what I used to call Telford New Town. I was surprised to be called for an interview, but accepted the invitation, with the intention of using the day as interview practise. If I were offered the job, I would decline it. Simple. At the end of the day, I was called into the headmaster's office, and he offered me the post. My resolve failed, and I asked if I could have twenty four hours to give him my answer. He said I had to give my answer there and then. In a panic at a vision of unemployment, starvation and destitution, I accepted the post.

When I got back to Swansea, we had a celebratory meal with my house mates in Brynmill to toast the news that I was entering the world of salaried professionals. I cried the whole evening. The following day I wrote a letter to the headmaster saying that I had changed my mind. I didn't mention anything to him about the tall dark handsome poet with a brown velvet voice.

That summer Nigel asked me to move in with him. My chapel-going parents, although they liked Nigel straightaway, were not too keen on the idea of their daughter 'living in sin'. In retrospect, I can only marvel at the fact that Nigel asked me to live with him. Domesticity and home-making were not really his forte. In 'Note with Bluebells' he talks of the 'littled world of two'. And in 'Shirts', a love poem, the husband nevertheless is looking for a sort of freedom:

> She hangs out his shirts,
> and the air they breathe
> fills them with flight:
> his gentle arms rage
> flailing at the sky,
> scratching and clawing
> to catch up with the wind.

As a writer, he guarded his solitude, and although he had a number of significant, and some not so significant, relationships with women over his life, I was the only one he ever lived with, and I am grateful for all the years we had together.

And so began what can only be described as an idyll. The Nissen hut was situated on the land of the farm at Kilvrough near Parkmill in Gower where Nigel had grown up. It lay at the end of a grassy track, and the views were uninterrupted by any form of human habitation. Behind the hut, screened by trees, was Kilvrough Manor, used at that time by Oxford Education Council. To the side were views over the fields of the farm, and out of site, the farmhouse where his brother Martyn and his wife Jan lived. And to the front the most glorious views over the deer park (although there were no deer by then) over to Cefn Bryn in the distance.

In his book on Gower, Nigel describes the tower folly on a field on the farm, and he says: 'As a romantic teenager, I used to fantasize (with W.B. Yeats in mind) about restoring the tower and secluding myself there – with wine, books and a beautiful girl – to compose poetry.' He got the wine, the books and the girl, and although he never quite made it to the tower, we were only a field away.

The Nissen hut's official name was Lawn Bungalow, but Nigel hated that name, thinking it smacked of all the bourgeois twee-ness of what he would call 'white settlers'. And so he changed the name to Llwyn-y-fferen, but the Welsh name never really caught on. Years later, when he was researching his book on Gower, he asked his brother about the names of the fields of Kilvrough Park Farm, and it turned out that The Lawn was the name of the field where the nissen hut stood. I must admit I always preferred the name Lawn Bungalow. The contrast between the suggested grandeur of the name and the actual building was enough to make me smile. Nigel also changed the spelling of Kilvrough to Cilfrew, but later he reverted to the original spelling after Harri Webb suggested that Kilvrough might be an Anglicisation of *cil-yr-huwch* (retreat of the sow) – the sow being Llywelyn Fawr (Llywelyn ap Iorwerth, Prince of Wales; c.1173-1240), known for the swinish ferocity with which he and his warriors would rout up everything that stood in their path.

The inside was basic. Under the lino floors that went through most of the building, you could often hear the crunch of woodlice underfoot, desperately seeking a safe haven. Apart from the main room, it was very cold in winter, and in the mornings my facecloth was frequently frozen into the shape of the side of the bath. But the crowning glory and the charm of Lawn Bungalow was the main room, which served as a sitting room, a basic kitchen, and Nigel's work place. There was an open fire with a bread oven at the side. We often used to cook sausages to a crisp and brown perfection in that oven. I can still see them, hear them sizzling, and taste them. And as well as an assorted collection of easy chairs, there was Nigel's table, which Adrian Mitchell would later call his 'making table'. It was large enough for his 'mind maps', and it was positioned in front of the window that looked over the fields to Cefn Bryn in the distance.

When the money was tight, we turned to making home brew. Nigel's beer brewing production was almost industrial in scale. There was always a pint ready from the 'beer sphere' for thirsty friends. It became known as 'Jenkins' Thump', and it floored many an unwary boozer.

My attempts at wine making were less successful. There was a particularly disastrous batch of dandelion wine, which came in handy as a toilet cleaner. Elderberry wine was my forte, although the brewing process did not always go smoothly. I remember one time that I put the demi-john at the top of the airing cupboard to keep it warm. The hot water tank in the airing cupboard was heated by the open fire in the sitting room. We had no means of controlling the heat, so if we had a raging fire, the water in the tank would gurgle, boiling furiously. Unfortunately on this occasion, it got so hot that all the elderberry wine bubbled over, right over all the sheets and towels that we stored in the airing cupboard. In spite of this, I did mange some very good bottles of elderberry wine. I remember opening one bottle that we had kept until we moved to Mumbles. Even Nigel, whose capacity for drink was legendary, was surprised and delighted by the power of that elderberry wine. And it tasted like nectar.

Sometimes on cold winter evenings, we would drag the mattress along the drafty lino-ed corridor to lay it in front of the fire, and there we would spend the night in the warm glow of the dying embers. On several occasions, friends called in the following morning, coming in through the unlocked door, and would be bemused and slightly embarrassed to find us still lying there, when the 'Busy old fool, unruly Sun' had already woken most people.

One of the joys of such a relationship is that it heightens the senses and the feeling of *joie-de-vivre*. One morning, as I lay in bed and looked through the thread-bare curtains, I was aware of an other-light. Yes! It had snowed! I leapt out of bed, as excited as a small child, and ran naked down the corridor. At the door, I must have had a brief moment of thinking I must be sensible about this, so I donned my wellies, and grabbed Nigel's cap which was hanging on a hook by the door. And so out into the crisp virgin snow! Nigel followed bleary-eyed and took a picture of me, shakily, with my Kodak Instamatic.

It was a good place to be naked, without having to worry about the neighbours. One summer I was out digging the garden, again wearing nothing but a pair of wellies. But I was not as alone as I had thought... Nigel's brother Martyn was out riding the fields on his horse. Later, laughingly, he told me that he nearly fell off.

And so we settled into a sort of routine, one of lovers and friends who were totally comfortable with each other. Soon after the Telford debacle, I got a job teaching English at Olchfa, a comprehensive school some five miles or so from Kilvrough. I stayed there for two years and one long term before I jacked it in to follow my own creative path. When I used to leave in the morning, Nigel would be already coffee-ed and toasted and ready for a day's work at his making table. On my way back, I would often pick up a couple of flagons of Brains and a bottle of Choix du Roi, a perfectly quaffable *vin de table* with stars around the neck of the metal capped bottle. When I returned, he would still be there at his table with one of his 'mind maps' spread in front of him. These were made of six or eight pieces of A4 paper stuck together, and on this he would put all the ideas for the poem he was working on. I never asked him what he was working on, and he never told me, a sort of superstitious ritual similar to a woman not talking of an early pregnancy. I certainly never looked at those sheets. It was an unspoken agreement, just like you never look in someone's diary. But I sometimes had an inkling of what the subject might be. I can still see the snowdrops in a bubble-shaped glass on his worktable.

> I find them a glass,
> and on the worktable
> scattered with papers
> I place them
>
> It is enough.
>
> *   *   *
>
> Thin sun creeps
> upon the afternoon
>
> and the water warms,
> bubbles sprout

on the earth pale stems.

They'll die early, yes,
and drop no seed:

The year may live.

When the poem was finished, he would type it out, and then present it to me.

This was the only period in his life when he was really and truly a full-time poet, before the distractions of Trinity College Carmarthen, the *Encyclopaedia*, and the Creative Writing course at Swansea University. And it was at this time that he wrote what I consider to be his best poetry, certainly the poems that have become much-loved and anthologised – 'Where Poems Came From', 'Yr Iaith', 'Shirts', 'Circus', 'Snowdrops', to name just a few.

He was doing lots of poetry readings at this time, and I heard his poems so often that I practically knew them off by heart. I loved the way he could hold the audience in the palm of his hand. 'Yr Iaith' never failed to get a heartfelt response of appreciation and recognition, while 'How to get Lynched in a Bourgeois Democracy' would have Swansea audiences rolling in the aisles. His poetry of course had an unashamedly sharp political edge to it. In the wake of the failed devolution referendum in 1979, he wrote 'Land of Song'. He would loudly declaim the first line:

Oggy! Oggy! Oggy!

Invariably the response would come from some beer-inspired listeners:

'Oi! Oi! Oi!'

Nigel would pause dramatically, and then launch into the following lines:

This is the music
of the Welsh machine
programmed – Oggy! – to sing
non-stop, and to think only
that it thinks it thinks
when in fact it thinks nothing.

The oggy-chanting members of the audience would be left squirming in their seats, forced to reassess, through the force of a poem, what their Welshness actually meant to them.

He never had any intention of taking up the family businesses of agricultural auctioneering and farming, although farming and agriculture were the inspiration for many poems from this early period, and indeed remained a vital interest for him throughout his life. One of the poems from this time, 'Castration', famously floored a super-sensitive veggie at the Hay Literary Festival. Thankfully, the listener was brought round with the help of St John's ambulance. Nigel loved recounting this tale, and would chuckle mischievously with, it has to be said, a certain amount of boastfulness in recognition of the power of his own poetry.

* * *

This was just the beginning. We eventually moved to another shack, this time in Mumbles, and later we moved to a real house with a slate roof, brick walls, and not a whiff of asbestos about it. And 'Reader, I married him. A quiet wedding we had…', so quiet in fact that our marriage was Swansea's best kept secret for many years. And of course, we had our two wonderful daughters, Angharad and Branwen.

Sadly, when the girls were twelve and ten, we separated. I was hurt, of course, but in the years that followed I channelled my energies into minimising any hurt that the girls would feel as a result of our separation, and taking them through their teenage years, with all the worry, hard work, but also great joy, that that brings.

But this is a story for another volume.

* * *

In the last six weeks of Nigel's life, between the diagnosis of pancreatic cancer and the end, he seemed to improve as a human being. He showed me more love and affection and gratitude than he had done for many years, and we were able to become close again. As a family, the four of us spent some all-too rare but indescribably precious hours together. No one could doubt the love he had for his girls, his 'small little tribe'. The three of us will remember and treasure those hours for as long as we live.

Nigel was a wonderful and special man, a unique human being. I feel so lucky and privileged to have been part of his life for so many years, and to have been able to give to him the precious gift of our two daughters.

I kiss yous,
kiss you as you fly.

Against the Vultures of Unthink

Daniel G. Williams

As befits a poet and essayist of Nigel Jenkins's undoubted skill, much good writing has been produced in the form of obituaries and remembrances since his untimely death on 27 January , 2014. Many have evoked particular conversations in which Nigel is often the listener responding, with that characteristic glint in his eye, to a tall story, an inappropriate joke, or passage of creative writing by one of his tens of admiring and appreciative students. Others have recalled the man brought up on a farm in Gower, '*dyn ei filltir sgwar*', or have rekindled that deep baritone voice in the mind's ear; a voice which – like a pint of '*cwrw* Felinfoel' – accessed areas that others could never reach and which, depending on the poem or passage of prose being read, could conjure dreams of buccaneering Bohemian restlessness on the one hand, or a deep meditative rootedness on the other. These are memories of Nigel cherished and shared by people of many backgrounds from Mumbles to Maenclochog, from the bars of Remsen, New York to the hills of Khasia, India.

But there is another aspect of Nigel Jenkins's life and work that we should never forget. For Nigel was a poet who, through the devastating choice of words, could cut through the blinding British-ness of our institutions, could expose the vacuousness of a bogus internationalism which has no space for Cymraeg, could lampoon our willingness to orgasm convulsively as 'Roddy fucks royal in Bahamas' and to celebrate the assimilationist, quisling, 'white man's Welshmen'. Like the African American poet Amiri Baraka, who died a few days earlier on 9 January, Nigel's calm exterior and expansive, generous, character, harboured a poet who could convey the anger and bitterness of nationalist frustration like few others. Jenkins considered himself one of the 'Idrisiaid' in his commitment to a poetry that spoke directly to different constituencies without 'p p p p p pseudo-experimental party turns/ designed to impress'. But when his critical intelligence was fully inflamed, Nigel's visceral anger would explode the formal, Georgian, confines of Idris Davies's verse. And he was able to focus his ire with a lacerating personal directness in a way rarely achieved by his more impetuous – but often equally irate – hero, Harri Webb.

While Jenkins recalled recently that 'the four to one defeat for devolution in the 1979 referendum [...] stunned many a patriot into numb silence', his own response at the time was to channel that shock into a poetry of anger.

> Ar hyd y nos, ar hyd
> y dydd – the songs, the songs,
> the hymns and bloody arias
> that churn from its mouth
> like puked-up S. A. –
> and not a word meant
> not a word understood
> by the Welsh machine.
>
> Oggy! Oggy! Oggy!
> shame dressed as pride.
> The thing's all mouth
> needs a generous boot
> up its oggy oggy arse
> before we're all of us sung
> into oggy oggy silence.

In advising a young poet to always ask 'Who needs it' of his or her work, Nigel was no doubt reinforcing the misguided view of some unsympathetic critics that Welsh poetry in English is conformist in its communitarian and social preoccupations. When Nigel's social critique was at its most powerful, however, his poetry of social purpose was also a form of avant-guardist intervention. Amiri Baraka, in his nationalist verse, targeted

> negroleaders
> on the steps of the white house one
> kneeling between the sheriff's thighs
> negotiating cooly for his people.

Similarly, Jenkins revised the nauseating paeans to George Thomas in his 'Tasteless Farewell To Viscount No' propelling himself onto the front page of *The Guardian* in 1997:

> O Death! For past misdeeds I almost forgive you
> Now that you've lightened our land of this load,
> The Lord of Lickspit,
> The grovelsome brown-snout and smiley shyster
> Whose quisling wiles were the shame of Wales.
>
> Queen-cwtshing, Brit Nat, Cymro Da,
> The higher he climbed the acider the rain
> He pissed on his people
> As he stuffed them with Prince shit
> And cheered as the voice of Tryweryn drowned.

Shortly afterwards, a leading Anglo-Welsh critic wondered whether Nigel Jenkins might be one of the bards 'appointed to celebrate the opening of the Welsh Assembly', noting that he had 'the right idealistic concerns and a broad, vigorous voice'. Upon reflection, Jenkins was disqualified from playing such a role due to his 'odd views'; 'he is consumed with animosity for the English, whose evil hand he sees behind every unwelcome development'. Several generations of English students and colleagues inspired and encouraged by Nigel Jenkins may wish to disagree. While Nigel was firmly of the view that Wales had lived for 'more than 700 years as England's first colony', he was convinced that the form of our nation's future independence would be conditioned by the way in which England, 'long blinded by the dazzle of empire, reawakens to the particularities of its own nationhood'. Jenkins's hope was 'that the version it chooses for itself is the England of Shakespeare, the Levellers and the Diggers, Tom Paine, William Blake, Charles Dickens, *The Guardian*, Adrian Mitchell and P.J. Harvey, rather than that of the football hooligan, the English Defence League and the British National Party'. Indeed, when the target of his poetry was 'England', Nigel tended to adopt a comic or satiric mode, as in 'Creation' where, in revisiting an old joke, he has God confess that the unsurpassable beauty of the Welsh landscape and people and superiority of our beer is compensation for the neighbours with which He's lumbered us.

Nigel Jenkins's attitudes to most people and places was never simplistic. In meditating on the historical significance of the missionary movement in his magnificent travelogue *Gwalia in Khasia* he was led to wonder:

> *could we not contrive, on this blue tormented planet of ours, some functioning convergence of the Universalist and Relativist creeds, a new humanism which understands and celebrates the huge differences that exist between peoples – an aspect, surely, of the sustaining variety of terrestrial life as a whole – at the same time as it nurtures belief in the existence of some shared humanity? One more tall new order for these dark days, and the stuff, no doubt, of dreams...*

Nigel lived that dream as a nationalist who embraced universalism, and as an internationalist with a profound, poetic, appreciation for cultural difference. This did not equate to a woolly liberalism, broadly tolerant of all traditions and lifestyles. Regimes which were seen to challenge human diversity and to regiment life were the subject of powerful critiques. The 'America' of of his poetic sequence 'Circus', for example, is a nation brutalised by war. Animals are brutalised as are women. A circus man and Vietnam veteran recalls sending a favourite stripper 'a gook ear' but hears nothing back 'the whole war long'. His sense of disappointment is alleviated at a strip club as 'Labia major gets down, takes his dollar in her cunt'. This takes place in a 'clean town' where billboards celebrating 'America the Proud' co-exist with signs claiming 'I made Linda Lovelace gag!' In the world of the circus, pornography, war, nationalism and capitalism fuse into a crude, debasing, if heady, mix. The America depicted in the sequence has no redeeming qualities. If the US is represented in general terms as an all consuming capitalist circus, the few specific voices in the poem are all complicit with the debasing system; circus workers direct their visceral prejudices at women, animals, the elderly and the disabled, and the voice that comes from beyond the circus world is that of a redneck who clothes his bigotry in piousness:

> No fags, no niggers,
> no mother-fuckin reds: we gotta
> way roun here a keeping things clean,
> y unnerstan me, boy?

In the face of this relentless process of dehumanisation the poet tries to remind himself that

> ...my name
> is Jenkins, my country Wales

but these badges of identity are wholly irrelevant in a life reduced to

> flogging nuts n
> Cotton candy – these are the facts.

If his boss recognises that Jenkins's accent may prove useful in selling 'sno-cones', he's ordered to tell the punters 'you're English – who the fuck's heard of Wales?' In the hierarchy of global powers America is the 'greatest land in all the free world', obliterating the existence of minorities.

But, characteristically, this is not the only America in Nigel Jenkins's writings. He writes movingly of the sensitive responses of American students when, as a tour leader, he takes them to visit Tryweryn.

The Americans are shocked that this entire community was wiped out – not in medieval times but as recent as the 1960s – so that Liverpool Corporation could build a profit-making reservoir. They find it difficult to believe that although the Welsh were united, for once, in their opposition to the plan (with the exception of George 'Viscounts Against Devolution' Thomas and one or two other quislings) they were powerless to stop it. 'Everyone in Wales should come and take a look at this sad place', said a student on one of our visits. Yes, indeed.

The American students' sensitivity also manifests itself in the distress that they express 'at the churches up for sale and the chapels turned into curry houses bingo clubs', while 'we natives' are 'zonked on a newer trinity of Shopping, Telly and the Holy Lottery, and perhaps less inclined to sorrow at the sight of a corpsed Bethel'. Jenkins' America is thus not consistently the cesspit of pornography and violence depicted in 'Circus'. American popular culture in the form of 'pop music, blues, country and jazz' reappear as sources of inspiration throughout Nigel's work, such as when Brad Mehldau's piano is evoked as a backdrop to the hallucinatory landscape of 'Hotel Gwales'. Elsewhere, it is the addictive generosity and enthusiasm of the people that strike the poet while touring the US with the Welsh-language poets Iwan Llwyd and Menna Elfyn, and the 'complex, enviable variety' of the nation. The 'Welsh-made town' of Remsen, New York State, is remembered fondly in 'A Round for Remsen' as 'brotherly' and 'quietly diasporate', words which evoke an America quite different to that of 'Circus'. Even in 'Circus' itself, the use of invective is reminiscent of a Scorsese or a Mamet, the range of voices reflects the dialogism of pop or jazz, the voyeuristic sexuality draws on the visual grammar of pornography, the shift in registers from the demotic to the meditative reflects the switching of TV channels. A great deal of the linguistic vitality and force of the sequence derives from the very popular culture whose debasing, corruptive influence is being exposed at the level of content.

The real ire and profoundest, unsparing, anger in Jenkins's poetry is directed at the assimilationist elements within Wales itself. In 'Never Forget Your Welsh' Wynford Vaughan Thomas, 'Sir Neddy Seagoon' (Harry Seacombe) and Max Boyce are our heroes, appointed by the 'sheep' of a Wales populated by

> vultures of unthink
> Thatcher their queen
> came to the Patti
> told us
> go
> Maggie Maggie Maggie
> Charles and Di
> orgasmic grovel
> glee-faced serfs no
> tongue like a Taff's
> for lavish licking of the royal arse

This thread is picked up in 'Colonial', a poem based on the 'ten months I spent bumming around Europe and North Africa in the early 1970s', an experience seen later as the 'clincher' in a long process of reclaiming a 'Welshness' that Jenkins describes as having been denied him during his childhood and education at an English private school: 'Most of my family had been in anxious denial of their Welshness for two generations. The Meurigs, Eluneds, Eiras and Dilyses of my grandparents' era had given way in my parents' time to names such as Ian, Roger, Noel and Rowland, as chapel and the Welsh language had been abandoned for church and English.' What he encountered in Morocco was a generation of young pimps – 'Wan'/ maybe fuck Moroccan chick?' – selling off their women, language and their culture in assimilating to an American norm.

> They old, no good. Me
> No Moroccan, me
> English, me American freak.

The poem's final two lines are reminiscent of Harri Webb's poems 'Israel' or 'For Fanon', but rather than following Webb in overtly spelling out the terms of the comparison, Jenkins merely asserts

> Yes, sometimes, David bach,
> Sometimes Morocco springs to mind.

There is much, of course, that is problematic in such comparisons. At its weakest Nigel's work replays an all too familiar form of anti-Englishness in which the Welsh 'we' tend to be the peripheral, the dispossessed, the struggling dissenters, mavericks and critics, while the English or American 'they' represent the power of empire, capital, the State, the condescending and the exploitative. When I discussed this with him, his response was that there are times of conflict and crisis where these sharp binaries are usefully, and necessarily, deployed. 1970s America was one such time. Now may be another. Our current moment seems characterised by a 'common sense' and 'mature' neo-Victorian Britishness, manifested by our Labour MPs being cheer-leaders for 'one-nationism' while our writers seem delighted to have attended a reception for poets at Buckingham Palace. Nigel Jenkins expressed his withering contempt for the former and would have had no time for the latter. I will remember him, *yn annwyl iawn*, as a principled socialist and (inter)nationalist who recognised that 'it is/ good to have/ friends' but 'it is/ necessary/ to have enemies'.

How else?

David Hughes

(In memory of Nigel Jenkins)

I don't think I saw him run.

Always the careful, measured tread,
a farmer marking out his land;

and on the bike, his legs would push
that same deliberate measure.

How else to get the rhythm right?

How else to find a snowdrop
or see the clouds transforming?

'A gathering of atoms'*

Margot Morgan

As my grandchildren play around my feet, I remember a day last July that Tobias (aged two) and Nigel spent on Langland beach, digging boats in the sand and wrestling the tide as it invaded to wash them away. Nigel was a man full of joy, full of play, full of love.

Through this past year, as we'd walk together rediscovering Gower for his last book, he would consume the landscape with his eyes in a way I had never seen him do before, as though he knew intuitively how vulnerable he was.

A few nights ago I dreamed that we were dancing (he didn't much like to dance), his face aglow, his feet floating in midair, his Popeye giggle in my face, his irresistible laughing eyes sweet with affection. In Pennsylvania today, on a visit with my family, it passes through my mind that the best time to phone him is mid-afternoon, but that Chagallian visitation is the only kind of call I'll get. It's raining here, thunderstorm season is in. These torrents and black skies are a far cry from the small rain that falls sometimes on our homes in Swansea, where we would lie quietly listening to the *glaw mân*, as Nigel taught me to name it, and often he'd recite this poem by anon:

> O western wind, when wilt thou blow,
> That the small rain down can rain?
> Christ, that my love were in my arms
> and I in my bed again.

Nigel encouraged my interest in the history of Wales that I had left as a small child, and where I chose as a young adult from the USA, to make my home. He treated me, over our years together, to cultural riches and heritage, taking me to concerts, festivals, readings and book launches including the annual Dylan Thomas Festival in Swansea. He walked me all over Wales, teaching me as we went, his mind always full of the people and events that shaped the landscapes. He taught me to proof-read and then asked me to proof his own manuscripts. He was delighted that I took a keen interest in his work and encouraged me to undertake my masters in Welsh Writing in English, helping me with the challenge of juggling a family with a full-time job and study.

Nigel will continue to mentor me through the gift of his writing that he left us all and through my memories of his measured calm, his generosity of mind and heart, his wit and dedicated care. He was resolute in his commitment to his work, to his family, and to my family and me. He was a wonderful father and he supported my children too in their endeavors; he regularly spoke on the phone to my mother in Pennsylvania, sending her books that he thought would interest her, and kept up-to-date even with my ex-mother-in-law's health, visiting her with me when he could. He was considerate always and conscientious with his colleagues and friends. His lamb and pheasant dinners were legendary and he loved to host his friends and our families to three course dinners and BBQs where he would not allow our cups to be empty.

He would book my diary up to six months in advance, and diary booking events were often an excuse for a mini-party when we'd take turns playing DJ and share a good bottle of red wine. No matter how tired I was, he would rejuvenate me one way or another. He had irrepressible energy and was a meticulous planner, naming me for the honeymoon years of our relationship the 'late' Margot Morgan. That magic time lasted for over three years, and settled then into a steadiness only ever troubled by our living in two homes, an arrangement that I disliked. A couple of weeks ago, I went to sit on the wall in Caernarfon overlooking the Menai Straits where we spent a starry evening talking over our beer, about politics, the beauty of the sea, our families, time and space to work, how rich we were (something we told each other often), rich beyond measure. He called me his *compañera*, and I am grateful that through our last few years together we resolved our only problem; I know that, to quote Carolyn Leigh, the best was yet to come.

Tomorrow at the shore in New Jersey I will think of my love and how by this time in May, if he had been with us, he would have coaxed me into the icy waters of Rotherslade, and, maybe I'd swim.

I have kept a few texts that Nigel sent me in the weeks before we lost him:

15 Dec. 2013 05:01
You're wonderful. Best lover and support a man cd hope for.

22 Jan. 2014 17:25
A nos da i ti, my gentleness n hugely considerate love.

---

*Taken from Nigel's poem 'Here Now' (*Hotel Gwales*, 2006).

Botanic Gardens, March 1st, 2014

Janet Dubé

white clouds in blue sky,
white water in cascades,
white snowdrops in thousands:

walking through the snowdrop
festival, I think
of the snowdrop poet

and here they are, under
beech trees, on steep
river banks; in memories.

Savouring the Occasion
Nigel Jenkins' achievement in haiku

Steve Griffiths

Since the death of Nigel Jenkins, many people have understandably celebrated an earthy, rollicking, political identity, as well as a generous man and an insightful writer in several spheres. The man and the poet had a quiet eye for the pivotal moment and the telling non-event that is connected to where the politics came from – grounded observation from somewhere deep inside that was a part of him from pretty young. There was a resolution about him, in two senses of the word, that often gave his work, and his presence, a still centre.

The haiku was a vehicle for that quality of attention of his. In this essay I will argue that Nigel's haiku form a significant body of work in themselves – not a diversion from his more substantial work, and certainly not trivial: a distillation of qualities which he wore lightly, and as one with a kind of strength that was characteristic of him. His characterisation of the nature and development of the haiku in his short 'Afterword' in *Blue* (his first book of haiku, indeed the first full individual collection of haiku in Britain, published in 2002 by Planet) – his tribute to the possibilities of the form – could serve as his own epitaph:

> *It may be, still, that the haiku lives most fully in nature, for whatever its subject it never allows us to forget that we, no less than that spider or this droplet of water, are part of the living cosmos. But the haiku has moved effortlessly into the street, the factory, the office, the airport, and may cast its wise, forgiving eye on almost any aspect of modern life.*

Nigel is an alert poet – and I make no apology for shifting between tenses as I write about him: it is too early to do otherwise. The haiku is about encapsulating consciousness, and letting it fly, in a few syllables.

It can only demonstrate this capacity through practice: where words earn trust and make a connection by enacting the moment, embodying, fleetingly, what's behind the words, in a way that resonates.

His 'Afterword' expresses this eloquently:

> *The haiku encourages us to make distinctions and enjoy contrasts: to appreciate the little, neglected, 'irrelevant' things we routinely edit out of our busy lives as unimportant – what Wordsworth called 'seeing into the life of things' – as well as directing us towards the ineffable sweep of the night sky and the awesome interior spaces of the atom. It cultivates the Zen ideal of according an object the kind of attention that enables us not so much to look at it but to look as it.*

The practice of engaging with the moment is superbly achieved by many of Nigel's haiku. This one captures the act of waking up and forming a thought up from his fingertips, a human thought in the darkness:

> a drop on my hand
> from the bedside table – so,
> the cracked glass leaks

As an evocation of the dawning of a thought, a deduction, with the Japanese 'fewest possible strokes of the brush to suggest a whole world' invoked by Nigel in his 'Afterword', it has an almost microscopic perfection in its portrayal of the human animal waking and calculating. His use of the demonstrative 'so' is surely a knowing, teasing reference to a terrible cliché. The last five monosyllables deliver a limpid precision.

I will shortly discuss the breadth of scope of this quality of attention, but I would like first to say something about Nigel as a political poet of great range, which came to include the haiku – or rather, the haiku included the politics, one part of the air he breathed.

The seeds of this journey are there in his early poems. One of these has stayed with me as a touchstone for most of my writing life. It's a poem about masculinity, one of his set of poems about growing up on a farm; about rite of passage and its refusal. It demonstrates one of Nigel's defining qualities, that he questioned the assumptions and rituals we grew up with, with an uncomfortable clarity, for him and for us. It's a moral quality, but it's a temperamental thing too: he could not help an inconveniently challenging gaze, one that looked behind inherited or lazy assumptions, to the end of his life. I still believe that his first book announced a moral intelligence which in combination with his emotional intelligence remains unique in English-language Welsh poetry, not to mention British poetry. The compassion for the animal in *Castration* ('Song and Dance', 1981) is searing: but so is the compassion for his younger self:

> They sat him upright,
> like a man for barbering, and I felt
> in the warmth of his purse
> for the tubes.....
>
> With all that sky-wide bawling –
>   sound his throat
>   was never made for –
> some nerve in me was severed.
> There were words about
> that weren't to be trusted.

It's those last two lines that have particularly remained with me, and that compassionate knowledge that we are coerced into doing things that are not right for us: a knowledge he seems to have borne witness to throughout his writing life. Truth to himself remained with him.

'Thrashing Day' in the same volume has similar qualities. One thinks of the line of Milosz: 'To think that once I was the same man did not embarrass me.' (From 'Gift', *The Collected Poems 1931-1987*, 1988.)

I think Nigel's work belongs in a long tradition of humanitarian scepticism, of a poetry that seeks moral integrity in authenticity, authenticity in integrity. There is a story to be written about where these qualities surface in English poetry (and a separate account of the part a different cultural and moral consensus has played in Welsh poetry both in English and Welsh – and the different forms and traditions of the latter, to which Nigel's 'Afterwords' to both his volumes of haiku refer).

Such an English history would include such poets as Sir Walter Raleigh's 'The Lie', Sir Thomas Wyatt (a poet of fear in a reign of terror), and some of Auden's political poetry. But I would set Nigel most meaningfully in an international context, among those few poets for whom the welding of irony, subversion and generosity were a matter of personal necessity and often survival. Miroslav Holub and Zbigniew Herbert were masters of the awkward squad, for whom a nod and a wink offered a subversion that could include many thousands of readers but was largely invisible to irony-free post-war East European authorities. Nigel's highly economical inclusiveness has similar qualities in a looking-glass world where minds and bodies are held in a marketised grip:

> just once, down all these
> aircooled aisles, the tasty stench
> of human sweat

Nigel would have been clear that this haiku is political. His politics were an affirmation in terms intensely physical and visual. Interestingly, the politics are rarely to the forefront in the haiku of this very political poet. They inform a world view, often with an infectious affability:

> windy demo –
> swatted in the face
> by a 'Peace' flag

Nigel, of course, put it better among the many insights of his 'Advice to a Young Poet' in *Hotel Gwales*. Rereading this wise poem confirms that its strength will last:

> The straight thrust, lethally honed,
> may cause, on occasion, creative offence;
>
> but for memorable action,
>
> slantwise is wiser,
> as is out from behind
> who knows what bushes.

Preceded by:

> Poems, au contraire – and not least in Cymru –
> have made many things happen.
>
> Word surgeons, speech architects:
> poets are among
> the language animal's makers of life.

Note the 'among'. One of the gifts of this draught of cold spring water is its sense of proportion about poetry:

> What songs, here,
> await their singing?
>
> And how, in this place, worker of the word,
> might you make yourself useful?

I cannot think of another poet who has the equipment to come near this expression of rhetorical self-knowledge. It is a grown-up skill that is needed at this moment in our culture. The death of Nigel is more than a personal loss to many.

The haiku in English still, perhaps inevitably, has an association with the exotic, derived in part from the picturesque introduction of oriental poetry led by Waley and Pound, who rightly knew they were on to something, and that something was lean and spare. More precisely, it is associated with the esoteric traditions of meditation and of Zen Buddhism, as Nigel's first 'Afterword' notes. But it derives from a consciousness that is not entirely foreign: in the 'Afterword' to his second collection of haiku, *O for a gun*, he makes an eloquent case for the kindred spirit to the haiku in 'Englynion Eiry Mynydd' (lit.:The stanzas of the mountain snow, twelfth century) as translated by Tony Conran in his Penguin *Book of Welsh Verse* – and the text strongly supports this.

I would like to suggest a connection too in the way the sound and feel of the line of poetry in English has moved over time. One quality of the haiku's extreme economy is the weighing of each syllable, and the spaces and silences between words.

I link this to Alice Oswald's brilliant introduction to Sir Thomas Wyatt's poems, which I believe places such a quality of attention in a much older tradition:

> *...the important question (for me) is whether you hear in Wyatt a hurrying, incremental kind of music [the regular, iambic beat that dominated English verse after Wyatt, and which caused editors to 'regularise' his lines – SG] or whether you hear something more to and fro and rewinding, like birdsong – in which case the poem's overall effect is mainly made of the turnings and spaces between phrases. I think these two ways of reading are radically, even meta-physically, different*

I believe that Oswald's re-evaluation of the history of momentum in the English verse line makes space for the idea of that quality of grounded attention in the haiku as bringing something back to a vernacular tradition which was lost. The 20th-century emphasis on attention to small things is consistent with this (attention to big things is another matter, which Nigel did not neglect, unlike many contemporaries).

His second book of haiku, *O for a gun*, begins with this:

on their backs,
the two plastic chairs
in a swirl of leaves

It is hard to write commentary on haiku without crushing them with banality; so I will try to present them in a context rather than discussing them in too much detail. Juxtaposition and dumb show are a critical tool which leaves something to the reader's imagination. To me, this haiku carries multiple suggestion, an air that encompasses a life in a place, in a way that reminds me of passages of Chekhov. This brings me to a thought of Raymond Carver, a poet we both admired, and his practice, in his last illness, of selecting short passages from Chekhov to be juxtaposed with his own last poems in a moving, valedictory celebration:

my love stirs and breathes and
sleeps again,

part of this world and yet
part that.

(Raymond Carver, 'Two Worlds' in A New Path to the Waterfall, 1989)

Carver was, I suggest, another step on Nigel's road to the haiku.

Returning to attention to big things as well as small, this fourth haiku in the second collection deploys his observation like a master:

not crying
– this girl with hand to bowed head –
but phoning

I find this an elegant and powerful haiku of contemporary anthropology (I told you that commentary could crush with banality): cultural critique, portraiture, primate physiology and behaviour and its interpretation, a tiny drama of empathy confused, and with that echo of Stevie Smith's 'not waving but drowning'. Effortless in effect, in thirteen syllables, rich, almost (and not at all) casual.

> only the blind man sees
> that the leaf we're handing round
> is a maple

For me, this haiku is a minuscule treatise challenging received perception, the last line a surprise, playing with anti-climax in a way that turns us back to the beginning, creating circular ripples. It's the light philosophical touch of the concrete.

And the next:

> over the rooftops
> a white plastic bag breaks free
> from the binmen

I take this as a riff on liberty – as seen by the binmen? The spectator? Unnoticed? But not a banner – a white plastic bag which has broken free from the binmen, provoking thoughts of low economic and social status, a metaphor of something everyday, unconsidered: there's a kind of transferred empathy in 'breaks free'. But the choice of subject is so marginal and unnoticed that it is almost stripped of meaning. Yet, there is a note of exhilaration in its freedom that makes the heart reach out. Of course Nigel will not have considered this in such leaden-footed interpretative terms. It's embodied in the haiku.

There is too an element of miniaturist autobiography in the book:

> the barmaid I once
> craved – creased now, like me,
> and double chinned

A poem of ageing and mating: much of what Nigel learned with the years comes together in sharp-eyed celebrations and laments. His first book of haiku, *Blue*, shares these autobiographical features:

> long enough in one town
> to notice the people's
> ways of ageing

Nigel's haiku world view is nothing if not inclusive. This is one of a number that trace the passing of time in the kind of striking way that seems obvious if only you'd thought of it – but you hadn't: the originality striking the reader with familiarity. Among these, there are moments that are now unbearably poignant:

> big skies moving eastward...
> so much life, twenty years ago,
> left to live

This is one of several haiku in which Nigel's last line, sometimes as short as three syllables, packs a transforming punch, the last drop extracted from the form.

As is already evident from these examples, the autobiography is both of an individual and a community. In his 'Afterword' on the haiku in *Blue*, Nigel admits 'It may be useful, initially, to describe a haiku as a 'word photograph', but then qualifies what he sees as a limiting description: 'The haiku is much more exploratory ... and is profoundly engaged with depth, resonance and transformation.' One haiku illustrates this particularly:

> men at bowls,
> their bright spheres bustling
> among patient shadows

'Patient' is masterly. Time, and indeed mortality, is never far from these fragments. But then neither is sex. In *Blue*, particularly, there is a joyful accumulation of erotica:

> her new varnish
> delivers me,

as we
make love, into
a stranger's hands

And:

she leaves the bed to douse
the yowling tom; the humans
then make love

Throughout all of this, there is celebration of the weather and the natural history of Wales. It gets everywhere, never out of place:

long love
in the white high room;
gulls out sailing
the slow blizzard

Nigel luxuriates in all of the senses, as in this haiku of the ordinary domestic life:

fresh runners on the boil –
the house filled
with sperm-sweet savour

It's Proustian, with a democratic savour of the kitchen. At times he's capable of sweeping cinematic narrative suggestion – here in fifteen syllables:

glass from the crash
swept with confetti
to the side of the road

Perhaps Nigel's masterpiece of concision is the title haiku of *O for a gun*:

> gull hooked, trailing
> from its beak a yard of line –
> o for a gun

As we have seen, he had a lifelong and strongly held opposition to violence. I found myself weighing this in comparison with poem xxi of Heaney's 'Squarings' in *Seeing Things*, 'Once and only once I fired a gun'. At twelve lines, Heaney's poem seems to say all it needs to say in a way that is conclusive, though it too opens out, in a profoundly different, fully articulated way:

> The target's single shocking little jerk,
>
> A whole new quickened sense of what rifle meant.
> And then again as it was in the beginning
> I saw the soul like a white cloth snatched away
>
> Across dark galaxies and felt that shot
> For the sin it was against eternal life –
> Another phrase dilating in new light.

It is particularly satisfying to hold both poems in the hand: how is Nigel's 'opening out' different? The haiku has an extensive and somehow dynamic hinterland which is precisely not articulated but suggested: the clash of species in the search for food and 'sport' (like gulls to wanton boys), Nigel wanting to put things right, the unintended, careless cruelty, the horror of the pain sparely described – and the explosive irony in *O for a gun*. Perhaps I get too far into this, but there is even something painterly – or more appositely cinematic – about the 'O'. It is an 'O' of horror, as well as an important aspiration to put things right. This is reinforced by the book cover design by David Pearl, where the 'O' echoes roundnesses in the gun, a Peacemaker rifle, 1870s USA, 'the gun that won the west' as the acknowledgement puts it. One should not use extraneous material to interpret, or puff up, a poem; but this shows that Nigel knew quite consciously what he was doing. I admire the detail and movement of Heaney's poem greatly. But I cannot say that Nigel's fifteen syllables do less than Heaney's twelve lines. For me, it's a comparison that continues to reward.

Throughout all this, the reader will be clear that Nigel's touch is shot through with generous humour. He does not make much of it in his 'Advice to a young poet', but the jest is a joyful joist of his affirmations:

> two men who never speak –
> thrown together by ice,
> their hats scattered

And poignantly, again:

> 'cancer...' she enquires,
> noticing my weight loss,
> 'or a woman?'

There'll be a few of us in his generation who will relate to that.

Nigel was a late convert to rugby, and adopted it with gusto, a fact that he noted in delightful vein:

> a try! a try!
> Cymru yes! could swing it yet –
> the cats leave the room

Nigel had the suspicion of abstraction proper to a poet of our age, to any poet who had read William Carlos Williams. Yet in thinking through my increasing sense of the honour and pleasure of having been Nigel's friend, the abstractions roll up to the bar in tangible form: they glint and rivet in his poems. Justice, in a man of his politics: a justice never far from love, a juxtaposition that made him his own man, in the awkwardness of the world as he moved through it. Intelligence, throughout. Groundedness – a love of detail, and a sense of surprise to the end. And a weary lack of surprise at the endless capacity for self-renewal of human stupidity: and the capacity to nail it, and in its detail, almost to love it: almost, but not quite. Love, fatherly, sexual, the love of little quirks, of community, that social trust that lengthens the quality of life. And an informed love of green things and rock and sky and the living things in and around them, and of the marks of the history of human touch on them, until that touch begins to destroy and defile, when he finds it in himself to be pretty angry. The love of getting up in the morning and putting together a breakfast and planning a walk, or a gig, with friends. I for one won't see his like again.

I leave a last word to Nigel. I remember his 'making table' and the big paper he wrote on:

> to serve the poem
> you will need to be
> in a devotional trance;
> cast a spell perhaps
> with music or a walk or a stern espresso,
> then savour the occasion
> of pulling up a chair
> to the making table;
> savour the paper, savour the pen;
> raise a glass, if you like,
> – of water, coldest water –
> to the planet and this life,
> blow the muse a hopeful kiss
>
> and write.

Learning from Nigel

Jean James

Nigel Jenkins was my poetry and dissertation tutor over the course of an MA in Creative Writing at Swansea University (2012-2013). He introduced me to a new form that I had never encountered before: the haibun. Immediately I was captivated by this unique fusion of prose and haiku and committed myself to writing my dissertation as a series of haibun.

Nigel was always there in the background to encourage me. He had a way of sitting back and observing, and when I was with him my ideas often spilled out haphazardly; his pertinent questioning, astute references and patient responses enabled me to develop and structure my creativity.

In his final assessment for my MA, Nigel referred to Harold Pinter's *No Man's Land* and the words Pinter had asked to be quoted at his funeral in 2008: 'And so I say to you, tender the dead as you would yourself be tendered, in what you would describe as your life.' I want to tender my thanks to the man from whom I learnt so much.

Across the Water

Jean James

> brushing past
> the swallow's wing-beat
> my breath

My Aunt Kate is standing at the kitchen window. She can see right down over her farm fields to the brown trout river; her thick stockings are gradually migrating down her knotted calves. She is washing up, a job that seems like the labours of Sisyphus. But today her eyes are not on the land, instead, like me, she is mesmerized by the miracle of the telephone wires.

> promises
> a seed drifting by
> on the breeze

They are collecting again: this year's swallows. It is as if someone is threading a necklace of sapphires around the farm. First the crystal glint of one or two gems, and then, more and more, until the wires are beaded in blue. These were the same birds that Aunt Kate and I had greeted in May as the harbingers of summer. Then they had come twittering in, wrapped in burgundy bandanas, arcing away after the fuzz of little insects that jigged across the meadows, or ruffling in low over the river's throat. These were the same cowboy builders who had slung up the pimpled mud nests in the corners of the old barn.

By July the 'scaldies' gargoyled from the rafters, their mouths agape with want. The adults were frantic in response, swooping, wheeling, and banking like featherweight fighter pilots after the foe. I loved their slender manoeuvrings. On land their short legs lack grace, but in the sky they are transformed into something ethereal.

> sunlight on glass
> in the doctor's surgery
> stroking your hand

Sometimes the swallows would have a second brood as if aware of the fragility of their small lives. And then one day a summons goes out and here we are, Aunt Kate and I, as witnesses. There are too many blue-backs to count, all readying for that remarkable journey. This is a bird that weighs around twenty grams and has a brain the size of a pea, a brain that can store migration routes of over 6,500 miles and uses the sun, stars and familiar landscapes to find its way. 'Tomorrow,' says Aunt Kate.

I already sense the swallows' absence; their hearts are beating elsewhere. Aunt Kate feels my sorrow and turns from the sink for a moment.

'Do you know that sailors love getting tattoos of swallows?'

I shake my head.

'They think swallows will guard them on their voyages, that they're a symbol of safe return.'

I think about her words again the next morning when the bare wires swing, restless in the September wind.

> back home
> the chair still holding
> your shape

'Across the Water' won the British Haiku Society's Haibun competition in 2014.

Tail lights

Steve Griffiths

It's later than it was.
Time, the frozen constant:
the motion of a fleet
that cannot flex,
a seeming exoskeleton –
moist, frail life goes on inside,
the curve of time remote
beyond compute.

A friend is dead,
a friend I now need
to have known more.
How loss mangles the tenses.

This is a sign of age:
the warnings start to be redundant.
Like friends leaving an occasion,
their blue tail lights recede.

Stars in the expanding universe.

Staying in Hotel Gwales

Ivor McGregor

To read the poetry contained within this volume is to hear the warm and enquiring voice of Nigel Jenkins once again. A man who went out and met real life unflinchingly, even when it stung him sometimes, his work embraces that very life with all its joys and disappointments. What comes across so strikingly in this book and others by the same writer is Jenkins' appetite for observation, his love of nature, his keen sense of geographical place and history and not least his insights into the human condition through his own participation in life. This he records faithfully, sometimes with disarming candidness.

By no means an ivory tower modernist, Jenkins' poetry has an assured and self-transcending technique, craft acquired, ingested over many years and finely honed to the needs of his own unique voice. That voice was however already evident in the early work of the 1970s and his later maturity gave rise to the occasional jaw-dropper of a line that even Shakespeare would surely have envied, in the poem 'Handbook': 'Reopen the wound, that half-inch of white/ aslant the thumb's splayed mons'. Simpler and less abstruse than Dylan Thomas, Jenkins soon outgrew the influence (such as it was) of his early idol and he never seemed particularly intimidated by the long residual shadow. The other Dylan, Bob was probably more of a subtly persistent presence, not least in Jenkins' love for rock music which I think leaves a rough-hewn mark on his poetry, intangible to analysis, but somehow there if you savour it. In the terrifying poem 'Circus' (one of the great portraits of a nation) you can almost hear and feel the violent tooth-plucked strings of Hendrix' electric guitar through the shards of Jenkins' violent and judiciously foul language. This work, alongside the equally terrifying 'Warhead', Jenkins' exploration of the aftermath of nuclear war, summed up by an Owen-esque 'warning', seems to mark a turning point in his writing, for this observer at least.

Highlights for me in this particular 'hotel' are 'A Body of

Questions' (hauntingly read by the poet on his website) where Jenkins' latent and late-flowering interest in the sciences blossoms throughout a series of memorable and almost child-like questions. 'Poem for Andie', a touching and uncharacteristically fast improvised poem consoling a girl student in the aftermath of her recent break-up, not withholding a frank acknowledgment of his own older man's attraction for her, un-acted upon. Nigel, though he loved women, was a gentleman too.

Poems about people in his own life make for moving and compassionate reading. This being true art, the universal transcends the particular and occasional; Jenkins creates poetry out of his own experiences and sufferings which we can and inevitably expropriate for our own uses. This is a true, social poetry that speaks directly to us, much more so I believe than the hermetic pyrotechnics of Dylan Thomas. Jenkins would recite his own work in pubs, play music and distribute 'Penny Poems' pamphlets on the genteel Regency streets of Leamington Spa (including one of mine which caused him much mirth – 'Ding Dong Bell': 'What's a nice pussy like you doing in a well like this?').

Never once the patronising proselytiser, Jenkins brought poetry home to people, responding perhaps to some collective unconscious bardic instinct which was to flourish later during his own homecoming to Welsh identity, his rediscovery of Gower and the refashioning of his roots. Like the great composer Ralph Vaughan Williams, Jenkins intuitively understood the subtle need to be in some way congruent with one's natal environment, the cultural cradle which is ignored at one's peril. Jenkins, a Welshman, showed me the way to be un-chauvinistically English, in my own art as a composer as well as in life.

During the late '70s, Jenkins' abandoned his career in journalism to travel abroad in Europe and North Africa (I used to love receiving his postcards from Morocco) and he later joined a travelling American circus. A certain harshness entered his poetry at that point, the use of foul language as previously mentioned which resurfaces in *Hotel Gwales*'s 'In Vino', a strange and unsettling poem which seems to speak of a loss of communication, while the crass but honest rants of the winos next door perhaps refer obliquely to the titular absence of 'veritas'. This deliberate use of 'bad' language underlies Jenkins' sometimes grim honesty and fearlessness in his work. Bleak poems such as 'Mannes Ioye' explore sexual double-standards and hypocrisy, while the marvellously witty 'Punctuation Poems' respond to the daunting technical challenge of writing about a writer's basic signs in his own craft, in such a way as would enchant any reader. 'Semicolon', a poem typographically set dead centre in the book seems to know its place: 'I am the point of balance,/ a glass of iced water/ at the half-way hotel.' But despite his genial approachability, Jenkins became inoculated from quite early on in his career from the temptation to simply ingratiate his reading and listening public in spite of its very social nature – maybe because of that – nevertheless, it is one of those key developments for a writer which gives work strength and infrangible authenticity. For some, like Joe Orton, it took a prison sentence to attain detachment in writing, but Jenkins had already achieved that long before his own and marvellously typical prison sentence for cutting the fence wire at Brawdy. Composer Michael Tippett's mother claimed she was never prouder of her son when he went to Wormwood Scrubs for being a conscientious objector during the Second World War and I must say as a friend I was very proud of Nigel when he served a little time for his beliefs too.

Then there are the wonderful haiku, a form Jenkins mastered as comprehensively as the earlier Beat poet and novelist Jack Kerouac, which seem like subtle nuggets and epiphanies of contemporary 'nowness'. But the most moving work for this reader (who resumed a lapsed activity as a composer largely due to revisiting Jenkins' work for this book) is the final one 'Advice to a Young Poet'. Written surely during the last years of his career when teaching took place of what was probably a dormant muse, the wisdoms contained within this magnificent piece in a way sum up artistic values accumulated over the course of a writer's lifetime. Although Jenkins subsequently went on to write the wonderful prose books on Gower and Swansea (the former interlaced with exquisite haiku), the placing of this extraordinary paean to the apparently lost muse is perhaps significant and even unconsciously valedictory (as was the last year of his life) – situated intriguingly as it is at the coda of translations of other poets. This inclusiveness of the work of others, even on his own platform, while perhaps causing me a little irrational annoyance, in *Hotel Gwales* was so typical of the man's artistic generosity, whose genius was transformed into highly inspirational and facilitating teaching towards the end of his life. I remember the seeds of this generosity and I should know; I was brought up and educated by this incredibly lovely and occasionally flawed man who was no saint by his own admission. During that six-year window of blissful happiness in my life I absorbed so many values (and darknesses too) that I see re-echoing around the interior of *Hotel Gwales*. How beautiful, and yet how terrible too to find the residual legacy of a dearly loved one's life encapsulated verbally between these deep sea-blue covers of this book. My limited words while inevitably biased scarcely do the man credit. That we can leave to his masterly and moving output. Time alone will tell if Nigel Jenkins' poems will last; I think they will. Great I believe and know them to be, but how I wish we could have the man himself back.

To a Teacher

Benjamin Palmer

I knew Nigel Jenkins for just over a year, but I'm certain that his impact on my life is going to last far longer. I joined Swansea University's Creative Writing MA as a relative newcomer to poetry, yet Nigel's enthusiasm and encouragement enkindled my initially cautious curiosity into a true passion. During our tutorials he'd thrust piles of books into my hands, introducing me to a host of poets whose work soon came to inform my own. Among them was the Oklahoman Louis Jenkins who, although they were not related, would affectionately refer to his Welsh bard-in-arms as 'Cousin Nigel'. Others included the Japanese haiku masters Matsuo Basho and Kobayashi Issa, as well as many Welsh or Wales-based writers beloved by Nigel, like Tony Conran, Ken Jones and Christine Evans.

To the new arrival, poetry can sometimes feel more akin to a haunted mansion than a land of joyful discovery. With its convoluted, cobwebbed corridors, its rows of hallowed personages scowling down from high walls, not to mention all those strangely-named creatures – dactyls, spondees and anapaests – going bump in the night, the study of poetry can give the novice more cause for fright than delight. But under Nigel's tutelage, although learning the craft was as demanding as it should be, it was also an exciting adventure. Even the fiendish complications of Welsh strict metre, which Nigel jokingly nicknamed 'Welsh S&M', were more a challenge to be relished than a punishment inflicted. The fact that I still get such a kick out of attempting *cynghanedd* and *englynion* in English today – though nobody is forcing or, in fact, even asking me politely to do so – is testament to the enduring influence of Nigel's teaching.

On top of all this he was a lovely man: generous, down to earth and gifted with a mischievous sense of humour. I consider myself hugely lucky to have known and learned from him. He will be deeply missed by all those whose lives he touched, including, I'm sure, many grateful Swansea University Creative Writing students past and present.

Below a Gale

David E. Oprava

When Nigel Jenkins passed on a Tuesday morning I sent a message to Jon Gower that simply said, 'I feel it in the world and the weather.' The rain, squalls, wind, and general turbulence of the atmosphere that morning left most of Wales feeling as if we were under the ocean – below a gale, perhaps on a Gower beach, at the edge of the surf where the storm waves crash. All of us were trapped in this churning as bands washed across our small bricks and bones. I had to teach all day, just as Nigel had taught me for a number of years, and as the hours went by I felt a little ashamed that I was not completely there for my students. I was not there for the rest of the world either. I was somewhere out in the sea of thoughts who has riptides and currents of its own. Colours turned into feelings and sounds into memories as the day ebbed and flowed around its own particular axis mundi – that day's meaning, its soul. Hours later I came to the wine-laden conclusion that there was a palpable hole in this world and a glorious explosion into the next. I imagined all of his talent, grace, gentle kindness and ribald wit expanding beyond the speed of light, beyond the speed of life. And for the first time ever in my existence, I felt a little bit better about death. He now knows the answer to the question, 'why?' He is now infinite. Knowing this settled me in my cups, so close to sleep, and I did what Nigel had taught me. I wrote as clearly and simply as possible...

To Nigel

I'm jealous ... of a sort
now you know ... what comes beyond
each twist of your soul ... is gifted there
and makes me ... calmer to go

© David Oprava

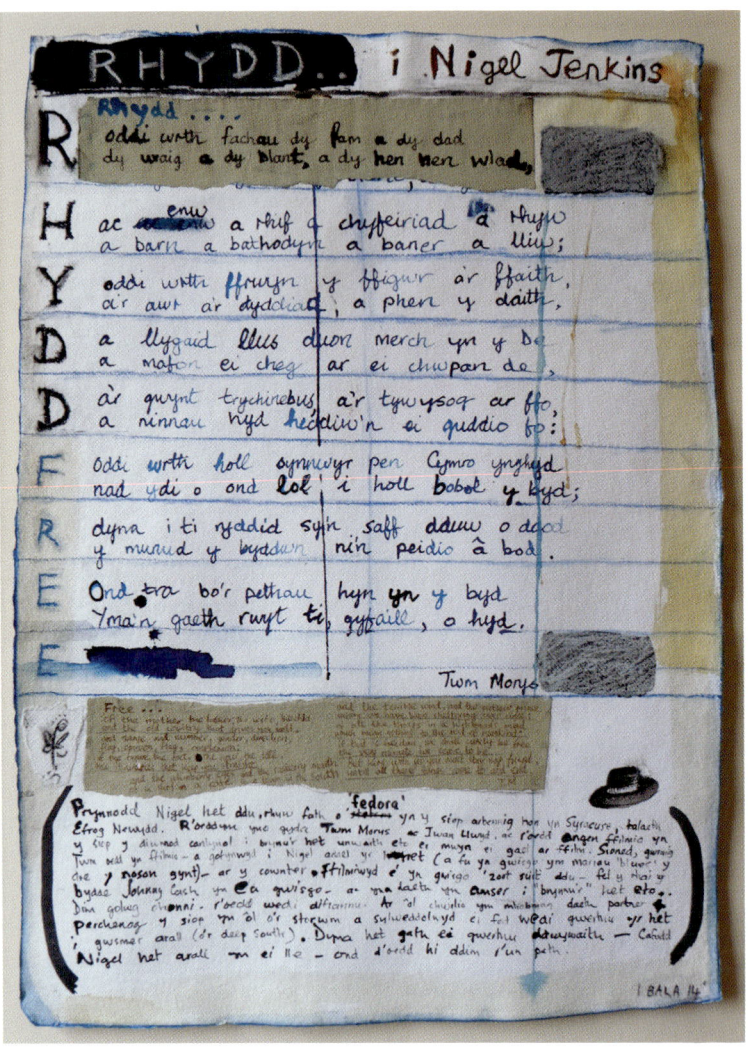

Rhydd/Free (i Nigel Jenkins), Iwan Bala, mixed media on Indian Khasi paper, 75x56 cms (2014). Poem by Twm Morys.
Purchased by Academi/Literature Wales and is on display at Tŷ Newydd, Llanystumdwy.

Time is What I Want

Janice Moore Fuller

When I arrived in the summer of 1997 to study in Laugharne, I stopped at Carmarthen station to pick up Nigel in my hired car so he could show me some sites. The previous spring I had hosted him, Menna Elfyn, and Iwan Llwyd for a reading at my college in North Carolina.

Nigel leaned in the window and boomed, 'Move over. I'll drive.' He jumped behind the wheel and off we sped. Carn Goch, Strata Florida, St Mary's Church and the yew tree at Dafydd ap Gwilym's possible grave, all the *Englynion y Beddau* – my first exposure to *cynghanedd*. On and on. Afterwards, I worried that, jet-lagged as I was, I wouldn't remember the details. He grabbed my notebook and jotted down every bit of the minutiae and more.

This was my first glimpse into his encyclopedic mind, a mind I was to learn did not lead him to be pedantic or condescending. When teaching with him at Tŷ Newydd, I was grateful he could be patient with the American students who joined us with their sometimes insular minds.

I always begin my poetry workshops back home with 'Where Poems Came From'. When I teach so-called 'British Literature', I ask students to read *Gwalia in Khasia* with its warning that all cultures need to guard against their colonial impulses.

I taught a fourteen-week course on Welsh culture for honours students at my college this spring. Nigel had offered to lead us during the Swansea-centered half of a trip during March. He died just weeks before our visit. Our last night, DnA (Delyth and Angharad Jenkins) played harp and fiddle for us at Morgans Hotel, weaving in some of Nigel's poems.

Last summer, in planning Nigel's role in the trip, he and I sometimes talked about mortality. As I approached the age my mother was when she died, I told Nigel I was remembering his poem about passing his father in their horse race. Nigel's email: 'At the age of (nearly) 64 (Will you still meet me? Will you still greet me?), time is what I want.' In September, as I prepared for brain surgery for an aneurysm, Nigel wrote, '*Solidarnosc*, Janice' – not yet knowing what awaited him.

Tributes

Mike Parker and Ceri Wyn-Jones

> *So many in Welsh lit over yrs have cited Nigel Jenkins as*
> *someone who had inspired, helped, been kind to them. That,*
> *friends, is success*

The words from Kathryn Gray plopped into the muddy swirl of my Twitter timeline. I nodded in silent agreement, though the thought did flit across my mind that it seemed a faintly random sentiment for a wet, workaday Tuesday. The sucker punch truth that it was a 140-character obituary only dawned a few tweets later.

At sixty-four, Nigel was too young to go. The fire still roared within; it burst out in his poetry, prose, politics, lecturing, psychogeography and music; it combusted all around him and brought light and merriment; it scorched even through the hallowed chambers of the *Encyclopaedia of Wales*, a project that ate seven years of his life as one of its editors, and which he wearily nicknamed 'Psycho'. His inability to stand the sickly cant of sanctioned public discourse brought both admiration and brickbats galore, none more piously hurled than when his bilious eulogy to 'Viscount No', George Thomas ('The Lord of Lickspit/ The grovelsome brown-snout and smiley shyster') landed him on the front of *The Guardian* and booed on the letters page of the *Western Mail* for months on end. As ever, he was proved entirely right on that one.

The last time I saw Nigel was at a hugely convivial event in Aberystwyth rugby club to mark *Planet* magazine's fortieth birthday. There was music, poetry, prose and speeches from a glittering cast that included Ned Thomas, Jan Morris, John Barnie, Gai Toms, Jasmine Donahaye, Damian Walford Davies and Samantha Wynne-Rhydderch. As compere of the evening, I'd come up with the idea of ascribing a different planet to each performer, a conceit that became distinctly strained on occasion (Jan Morris, suffering an injured foot, hobbled up to the stage after my introduction, cast me with a baleful eye and murmured, 'Well, I certainly don't feel very Mercurial right now'). While some were highly tenuous fits, there was no question which planet to give to Nigel: Mars, the red planet, named after the Roman god of war, the near neighbour that's fascinated us for generations, famous for its eruptions, its volcanoes and its elliptical orbit. I cringe to recall this now, but my last words before bringing Nigel to the microphone were 'So, is there life on Mars? There certainly is!'

And now there isn't. The sky is a far darker place without him.

* * *

Ceri Wyn-Jones

Many who pay tribute to Nigel Jenkins will be conscious of somehow doing justice to the man and his achievements, knowing it to be a gloriously impossible task. Many will also be at pains to deliver such tributes in terms as original and eloquent as those of the man they mourn, fully aware of the futility of such an undertaking. But all who do so will do so with tears in their eyes.

I first shared the stage with him at a poetry reading in Swansea in 1997 at an evening entitled 'Beirdd yn Dweud "Ie"/Poets Say "Yes"' in support of the campaign to establish a National Assembly in Wales. But it wasn't until I joined Gomer Press as an editor in 2002 that I really got to know him and came to appreciate how much more he was than the captivating verbal and vocal presence of the public performance.

Gomer will point to Nigel's great successes across a range of literary forms: the travel writing of *Gwalia in Khasia* (Wales Book of the Year 1995), the collections of essays like *Footsore on the Frontier* (2001), the poetry collections like *Hotel Gwales* (2006) and even the coffee-table collaborations like *Gower* (2009). But I will remember him too for his championing of new authors, along with his willingness to graft and campaign as part of a team, for example, as one of the three joint-editors of *Another Country: Haiku Poetry from Wales* (2011).

Yes, he was one of Gomer's greatest authors, but he was also one of Gomer's greatest friends.

Nigel Jenkins and the Welsh Union of Writers

Ifor Thomas

One of my first encounters with Nigel was at the Hay Festival, back in the late 1980s. We'd done a reading and I was enjoying a pint of champagne with Dylan Moran, thinking that this was real rock and roll. In those days you got paid in the bubbly stuff. Nigel came into the Green Room. He wasn't happy. I passed him a bottle.

'Champagne', he scowled. 'Do I tell my children to put it on their cornflakes?'

He spoke to one of the organisers who arranged for a cheque. 'These people, don't they realise that writing is real work and writers should get paid accordingly?' Then he gave me a grin and drank down a glass. 'Pay me the rate – then give me a drink.'

That's why he became the chair of the Welsh Union of Writers. His guiding principle was that writers should get paid the rate for the job. Hard today. Even harder then. But under Nigel's leadership the principle was established. He imparted to the WUW a gravitas it didn't deserve, pulled together an organisation of disparate egos. Somehow, his was a banner we could all rally round.

His last wish? To have champagne drunk at the graveside. 'What sort?' asked Angharad.

'Extremely good champagne', he replied.

After all, the work was done.

Forenames

Ifor Thomas

We shared English forenames –
vapid you described them
certainly not fit for a Welsh Republican.
I jettisoned mine
you stuck with yours.

With your leather boots
blue jeans and beard,
hair that flew,
big bear-hug man
the Khasi cowboy.

Your mount a bicycle
those wheels spun haiku
along the mumbles mile.
Poems of love and
lick-spittle scorn too

given life by the sounding board
of that voice. You, the one we
would have chosen
to read the declaration
of Welsh independence.

A last look at the wicker casket
Your name Nigel Leighton Jenkins.
Even now, you surprise me.

Post Funeral

Ifor Thomas

Days after, I still feel that bruise;
the bone of my left shoulder
carries a tender memory.

We hoisted you in creaking wicker
you sighing, grumbling in my ear
as we shuffled the narrow path.

The undertaker, bearing well
years denied you, directs.
The tape slides through my hands.

take the weight
lower him
together now

Feet first, swung under the slab.
This February morning, cold enough
to chill champagne.

You keep us there, dawdling,
never the first to leave
when there was a glass to raise.

And if that was just the wind
it might just as well have been you
enjoying a last laugh.

Before the earth
drops over you.

A Gower Man

Jane Fraser

It was on a balmy day in late September 2010. He was wearing his shorts which I would later learn was his summer uniform: his winter uniform, it transpired was his brown cardigan with the embroidered shoulders. To my shame, I didn't know much about Nigel at that time: I knew only that he was a farm boy turned poet, psychogeographer (though in truth I didn't know what this meant) essayist and travel writer, who hailed from south Gower – the 'other' side of Gower to where I'd lived ignorant of his work, in its north-west corner of Llangennith for over forty years.

In just over three short years working together, Nigel took me by the hand and led me through the MA course: at first, firing my imagination; then enabling me to say what I couldn't have said without him; through my final dissertation allowing me to morph my emerging writing into a hybrid of genres: travelogue, memoir, psychogeography (I'd learnt what it meant by then) and poetry, including haibun. Such was Nigel's take on possibility.

During this time our relationship morphed too, from student and teacher to close friends. We were around the same age and of course, shared Gower in our hearts. I remember our first conversation and me telling him that I lived in Llangennith. 'Ah, Langenny,' he smiled, using the dialect or 'Old Gower' form of the place name which carries with it associations of wild and unruly inhabitants of the past – and perhaps present – in this sometimes salt-lashed, sometimes sun-drenched, bi-polar place where land and sea collide at Wales's most western edges. The smile also questioned whether I was a now-wild or perhaps once-wild inhabitant of the village: it was egging me to spill the beans in my writing, if not about me, then about others who shared this space on earth with me.

And I would, for he instilled confidence and openness. He would later read my short stories and poetry woven with colourful local characters (fictional of course) who were attributed 'handles', sometimes affectionate, sometimes malicious, though always honest, by their co-inhabitants: Foot and Mouth, the chiropodist and barrister couple 'the only gays in the village'; Gareth the Goatman, the engineer turned smallholder who cultivated crops in his polytunnel, naked apart from his wellies; Nicky Nobrain and Colin Cabbage, no explanations necessary. Nigel had known 'Willy Harri' and 'Mrs Hearn' that he reminisced about in his writings. So, he knew my characters, such as Nicky Nobrain before they took form on the page before me. For Nigel knew most everything about Gower.

> *Nicky Nobrain, as he's called around here, starts yet another day. Again, he unfolds his sleep-aching body from the bed that turns into a table by day, groaning as he kicks open the door with his bare foot and pees last night's skinful of Felinfoel in a cascading arc from the top of the caravan step. Jesus Bloody Christ, he rages at the elements – a gust of wind off the sea is dousing his naked torso in a sticky yellow mist – a mix of salty horizontal rain and ammonia.*

At his death, Nigel was supervising me on my journey towards a PhD which focused on short story and a sense of place, which was, and is, of course, Gower. It would have been a 'no brainer' to have anyone other than him as mentor: we both expressed feelings of ambivalence towards Gower, in measures of loving and loathing which were about as unpredictable and fast-changing as the Atlantic fronts that passed through the peninsula. I wanted to convey a Gower that was not always pretty, more often gritty. He shared and encouraged that slant, motivating me to craft short stories where characters and plots would grow organically out of its distinctive geology and be shaped by its peculiar topography. Nigel knew the terrain: he was of its old red sandstone and its carboniferous limestone; of its wild and wet south-westerlies; its vanishing farms; its celebrity-endorsed beauty, 'too beautiful, perhaps, for its own good'; and the onslaught of tourism. He would have muttered irreverently at the latest in what seems an ad nauseum gush of marketing-led accolades, this one being Rhossili Bay voted yet again the number one beach in the UK. He knew the other side of this, often the dark side. He got what I wanted to say. As a man of Gower, of course, he'd get it.

But first things first. Nigel never stopped 'going on' about references to 'the Gower' as it was so often called on television, in the press, in advertising. It really used to irk him. As he says in his essay, 'The Lie of the Land' and the introduction to *Gower*, the wonderful book written by Nigel with photography by David Pearl in 2009:

It is not, please note, 'the Gower', common as that misnomer may be, but either 'the Gower peninsula' or plain 'Gower'. Quite how that erroneous usage developed is unclear. It has been suggested that when the people of the southern coalfield were largely Welsh-speaking they would refer to the Vale of Glamorgan /Bro Morgannwg as 'Y Fro' (The Vale), and that when they began making excursions to Gower they tagged an habitual 'Y' onto the peninsula, rendering it 'Y Gŵyr' (The Gower). It has never been known in Welsh as 'Y Gŵyr', but simply 'Gŵyr' – and that, unencumbered by a direct article in either language, is how Gower folk tend to like it'.

That's why in the course of our many email conversations (even his emails were works of art having such a distinctive voice) I got to share his private thoughts, especially about Gower. In July 2013 he responded to an article I'd forwarded him entitled, 'Let's move to the Gower Peninsula,' published in the money section of *The Guardian*, flagging up Gower as a desirable place to live.

'Yes, I saw this article. I wish almost everyone would stop calling it 'the Gower'. And the Hamptons tag doesn't help either!'

I noted the uncharacteristic exclamation mark (Nigel was not a fan of the use and over use of screech marks as he called them) so reflective of the strong sentiment he expressed.

Engagement with this complex reality and the issues of commoditisation of Gower's natural beauty were central to Nigel. He talked often of the breaking down of indigenous culture, the fragmenting of farms, the influx of second-home owners, dying communities. He says it well in 'The Lie of the Land':

In Gower I have watched a farm I love broken up into a cluster of meaningless plots for jaded city types who want a few acres on which to play the farmer. They harrow their fields not to keep the grass in good heart but to give their property the appearance of a neatly stripped suburban lawn; no one uses or remembers the resonant, history-laden names of the fields.

But Nigel did. He recalled them (and illustrated them in that distinctive scritchy-scratchy black-inked scrawl of his) between the pages of his book, *Gower*: Manor Field, The Beeches, Watkinses' Field, Deer Park, Cocklebushes, Six Acres, Quarry Field, Church Park … names and a time lost now to most, other than Nigel who now lies buried next to the church at St Mary's Pennard, adjacent to that very land that was once part of his father's Kilvrough Farm.

He made me realise that naming means so much, that there is so much story and history encapsulated in what we decide to call things: people as evidenced in his Wales Book of the Year *Gwalia in Khasia*, and closer still people and places in our own landscape. He knew his '*milltir sgwar*'; he knew his '*bro*'. He carried this knowledge of his patch with him until his dying day and he encouraged me (indeed all his students) to know their square mile, their bro, to know and reveal its truth in their own writings. He introduced me to the concept of 'found poetry' and I found story in the names of north Gower farms, many once belonging to my family, now long gone: Prysg, Freedown, Pen Mynydd, Sluxton, Muzzard, Lagadranta, Staffal Hagar. In the surnames of Gower's inhabitants: Groves, Beynons, Tuckers, Gordons, Lucases. And in places and landmarks: The Pancras, Tankey Lake, Hardingsdown, The Bulwark, Penny Hill, Sweynes Howes, Worm's Head and Burry Holms.

I tried to ensure my writing embodied the truth Nigel believed was so essential to tell. I remember only last March sending him an early draft of a story based on a fictionalised local farmer who sees his hopes and his dreams shrinking along with his land. Nigel seemed always to respond 'by return', often on Sunday afternoons, when he had put aside his quality time (sometimes I presume with a glass of good red wine in hand) to comment on my work. His comments were always constructive and often surprisingly positive, always expressed with humility, as was this, a typical Nigelesque crafting to the very first PhD piece I'd 'winged over' to him by email attachment (sometimes without having 'hitched up the cart' as he'd say when he'd get an email informing him of an attachment when none was present).

> *A mighty powerful piece of writing, Jane – this is real Gower, or an aspect of real Gower (he always italicised real), an unflinching honest and truthful slice of Gower life such as has never been written before. It's an important piece of writing... earthy and with a painful angularity.*

He knew then that I knew. We shared this painful truth about the peninsula which was part of us both. Perhaps he saw himself, or an aspect of a self he'd escaped, written in the character I'd birthed on the pages I'd sent. On seeing the marked-up version, I noticed that he'd inked in black a vertical black line right down the side of a certain paragraph – along with *WOW!* (plus another screech mark). I took this not so much as a seal of approval, but more as him empathising with the creation of my Colin:

> *Can't stomach it here in the kitchen where he sees his whole life playing out before him. There'll be a wife one day, a girl from a local farm, no doubt. She'll come here to this hellhole, this six-generation family home. She'll marry the farmer; she'll get Mother and Father in the bargain, all the days of her life, until they go, depart, join the other Reeses now silent, underground at St Cenydd's. There'll be a child, hopefully a boy, who'll grow, bring home a wife, brig forth a child. Colin sees himself slurping the soup, the uncouth manners, the big-bellied wife at the side of the table. There's a sound of silence. He doesn't want to stay in the kitchen; doesn't want to be out in the field, alone today. Anyday. Inside his head, the words are throbbing, on the cusp of saying: Father, I don't want to be a farmer.*

Father, I don't want to be a farmer. It was these few words which I think struck the chord and forced the vertical line. For these same words (or at least words similar, albeit in the past tense) hit me head-on in a recent rereading of the poem, 'Forty-Eight and a Half', written by Nigel when he himself had reached the age at which his father had died twenty-seven years earlier. I can see why Nigel had found truth in my work. There, forever on the page, is a public statement of a rapprochement between him and his father. But there is also perhaps a sense of guilt, a guilt that he carried, and admitted to, in his book, Gower: that he thought himself responsible, in part, for the demise of farming in Gower:

> There were furlongs between us. To your Brylcreemed Mohawk,
> The revenge of tresses sufficient to thatch
> An army of Gueveras; to the alleged music of Sir Harry Lauder,
> The orgasmitudes of Hendrix. I didn't want to be a farmer, Dad.

He didn't want to be a farmer, no; but he knew the farming lot and the farmer's lot. I remember way back in the first taught poetry module, writing a ballad that many in the workshop thought was written about events in the nineteenth or early twentieth century. Nigel said nothing, just smiled, that wry smile of his. He knew that despite appearances of sophistication and twenty-first century living, much of Gower was still corseted in time-trapped attitudes and expectations...

> But soon it came to issues new,
> to future children planned,
> to marriage and wealth management
> inheritance and land.
>
> Like barren fields in winter time
> poor Ann just could not bear
> a child for George she loved so much –
> there'd be no must-have heir.

Now in stepped Father, sharp and quick,
He'd have his way alright,
'That girl will have to go,' he said,
'if there's no child in sight.'

'No child: no farm,' the old man roared,
George feared he'd lose the lot.
And from Ann's arms, the girl he loved,
he bolted like a shot.

Although this ballad is simple in form and seemingly light in tone, Nigel understood the serious undertones: how farming struggled to survive, let alone thrive, in twenty-first century Gower. He understood the farming traditions that 'needed' to carry on – the eldest son as heir and all that carried with it. In his prose writing in Gower, he harks back to the Gower of the 1950s, when his farm, a typical mixed farm, like many others, represented 'not just a living but a way of life.' I wrote of a changed way of farming life in a poem which amused Nigel greatly; but as Nigel would, he also saw the sadness, the disappearance of the old ways and the sad realities for many farmers in Gower today, under increasing pressure to diversify or die as I titled the poem.

Nigel jokingly referred to me as, 'Gower's answer to RS Thomas' when he came to support me at my first set (he told me what the word was) at Swansea's Howl (formerly Crunch) in May last year. You never knew with Nigel's dry humour whether this was to be taken as a compliment or not. I recently learned from Nigel's colleague and dear friend, Fflur Dafydd, he didn't have a lot of time for dear RS. This did make me laugh.

Nigel encouraged me to pick away at the skin and expose what lay below the surface of our beloved peninsula: a striptease of the physical, historical, cultural, socio-economic landscape, through language, that removed the outward layers and arrived at the big reveal – warts an' all. And so I tried to write stories full of quiet revelations:

I should have seen it coming, seen it written in the blackberries, a pitiful and desiccated crop that clung too long to the brambles, well past the date that signified they'd felt the Devil's spit. Looking back, I suppose I should have read it in the holly berries that year: rare crimson flashes in what normally were just plain-ordinary hedgerows: waxy masses of dark prickles; gorse, sun-blaze long gone; dead nettles; and bracken, crumbling to dust in the hand. But then again, as my mother used to say, sometimes you don't notice what's under your very nose.

Mind you, neither did most of the farmers see it coming: Josiah Taylor, Barrastone, high up on Rhossili Down failed to see it in his lamb-filled ewes tucking themselves under the spike and spite of the blackthorn; Romney Tucker, Cooks Well, didn't see it in his pat-splattered Devons, facing east, knees locked, paused like commas in the grass; not even dear old Mr Vincent Bevan, Lower Muzzard, who never missed a trick, feel it in his waters or the crack of arthritic bones that cricked his body to forty-five degrees, crippled by the constancy of the on-shore south-westerlies.

Nigel always wanted to reveal truth. He kept talking about 'Real Gower' which of course was also the title of the psychogeography he had almost finished writing at the time of his death on 28 January 2014. This promised to reveal much in that unique way of his: a combination of fierce intellect, meticulously researched detail, wry wit and honest, unpretentious prose.

It was only last May I was privileged to mooch around the parish of Llangennith with Nigel, trying to add snippets of my forty years' experience here to his insightful observations. He was always observing and jotting in his journalist's short hand in the note book he carried, and advised me and all his students to carry. It was a hot, beautiful early summer day and Nigel wore his hat as we trod the bridle paths, condemned the caravan parks, rummaged in the crumbling ruins of the old abandoned village at Coity Green, and searched out the grave of one of Gower's other bards, the folk singer and 'prince of traditional balladry and exuberant mouth-music', Phil Tanner (1862-1950) among the rickety gravestones at St Cenydd's.

I have a lasting vision of Nigel that day, half-shrouded in unkempt grass, on bended knee, with his fingertips digging deep, trying to erase the decades of lichen that had obscured the etched lettering of the headstone. Sadly, the slate headstone had not been updated and did not reveal Tanner's name to 'record his presence there', only that of his wife, Ruth, who pre-deceased him by nearly thirty years. Sadly neither do I have the photographs that my husband took of Nigel that day, 'to record his presence there' either, as they too were lost in some technological process in which I have no interest at all. But the image will be everlasting. Like the Gower Wassail...

> We know by the moon that we are not too soon
> And we know by the sky that we are not too high
> We know by the stars that we are not too far
> And we know by this ground that we are within sound.

I will treasure forever Nigel's first draft of our day together, which I have in my possession. He sums up the sense of place that is the village where I have lived for more years than I care to remember. He captures its highs and lows, its characters dead and alive, its idiosyncrasies which he alluded to in his first mouthing of 'Langenny' and is summed up in his reference to a plaque on the wall of a new-build in the village which states: 'No one very interesting lives here yet!'

On the subject of interesting characters, he writes about one who has gone down in history locally: George Rees, a wonderful pianist and brother of Edward (he now immortalised in Eddy's café, Hillend) who was a former landlord of the famous – or infamous – King's Head Pub. Nigel knew George. I knew George. We have both written about him. Me in prose only last year when George became Richard:

> *That rain-drenched day when Richard finally came home, two weeks before Easter 1976, he saw the village as he thought he'd seen it in his youth. A romantic vision. Deserted. Untouched. Wild and desolate.*

George is present, too in Nigel's wonderful poem written after a Gower Poets' roadshow performance at the King's Head in 1977 when George, who had not touched the keyboard in weeks, took to the ivories after inspiration from the poets while 'insisting sadly that, unlike poets, he "had nothing to say"'.

Autumn leaves

No, they said, no – how
could you think it...?
when the man at the piano,
who had infiltrated
their cocktail souls,
informed them he had nothing to say.

And smiled. And played on,
back at sea perhaps
on the transatlantics,
outward by a thousand leagues
from his moneyed boredom,
the inherited pub
and farm of caravans.

The light he made in that
dark room – his fingers
feeling, feeling under silence
for petals, for string, the
perfecting note – held them
like rabbits...

But nothing to say:
before him a window, the black
pier of his piano pushing out
through the night: and distantly
stranger, one or many,
swaying armless in the wind...

They topped up his glass –

how could he think it?
He smiled, and played on.

Nigel came back to Llangennith again on yet another beautiful day: 5 July 2013 for Gwyl Mabsant (referred to colloquially as Mapsant Day from the Welsh 'sant' – holy, and 'mab' – son) the feast day of Saint Cenydd, founder of the church in Llangennith, its former priory, and the hermitage at Burry Holms. Recent years in Llangennith had seen a revival of the traditional way the festival was marked up until the early twentieth century, by displaying a somewhat comical effigy of a bird from a pole on the church tower. The said bird – as it goes – symbolises the legendary seagulls that saved the cripple Cenydd after he had been cast out to sea as a consequence of being born of an incestuous relationship at the court of King Arthur at Llougor. Apparently, the seagulls (along with a couple of angels and a miraculous breast-shaped bell known locally as the 'titty-bell') also cared for Cenydd during his youth spent on Worm's Head, and ensured that he survived and was educated as a Christian. Nigel knew all about Cenydd and Gower myths and legends though I don't believe for one minute he believed this one. It was the tradition he was interested in. And the way the local community marked the tradition. And when the celebrations were done, I sat with Nigel and other locals outside King's Head on the village green, looking up to Phil Tanner's last abode in Llangennith at Stormy Castle, and beyond out to sea.

He returned for the last time in the September for dinner here at Channel View. I have a vision of him and Margot coming in through the garden gate soaked to the skin. I hadn't heard a car pull up and he explained the reason: both Margot's car and his had broken down and they'd come on the bus – the Gower Explorer (number 116 or 118) – that characteristic single-decker with the distinctive yellow daffodil that has in recent years provided a much needed service in this rural outpost and enabled people to reach parts they might not otherwise have reached. A bit like Nigel.

One story keeps returning to me time and time again and illustrates how much Nigel seemed to know so many of the questions I had about

Gower. It concerns a strange white owl that I'd seen outside my house, three nights in succession last year. He'd seen a white owl too, a few years earlier:

> *Yes, we do have white owls, but I think they are relatively rare. One came from behind at dusk a few years ago as I was walking down Widegate Lane towards Bishopston Valley, its totally silent white span seeming to fill the whole lane as it then glided away down the lane in front of me. A truly magical moment. And my grandmother used to tell of a white owl she'd take my infant father to see in a folly tower at Kilvrough, sleeping on a ledge just below the 'battlements'. They were shocked one day when they found it lying shot – by some thug – in Highway Wood. I don't know the correct name for a white owl – Jon Gower would help you, I'm sure. Sounds to be as if there could be a poem coming on...*

And there was, and a haibun, and a story; there always was with Nigel's encouragement. He taught in a way that didn't feel like teaching and I learned in a way that didn't feel like learning – perhaps it was osmosis. Perhaps it still is. Nigel Jenkins, a man of Gower, a tutelary spirit in this place we both loved. He will go on teaching and guiding me as he guided countless students in his brief but beautiful life. His lines taken from 'Advice to a young Poet' will keep me on track and guarantee I don't write what he sometimes accused me of: 'desktop haibun'.

> Walk it, eat from it, drink its rain,
> Ask among its breezes
> For sign and sound
> Of those who filled their lungs here
> When the mammoth roamed
> Or when coal was a possibility of trees –
>
> Dis-cover your community.

Know your place. What legends and myths
have had their shaping here?
What stories, novels, histories?
And who have been denied a voice?

What songs, here
await their singing?

And how, in this place, worker of the word,
might you make yourself useful?

My last physical encounter with Nigel was in his office in December 2013 for my PhD tutorial. Always a man of consideration for others rather than for himself, he admitted unusually that he wasn't feeling 'too good' and we decided not to fix our next meeting, but keep it open. I made a note of this in my jotter: Nigel Jenkins next meeting? A blank page followed.

As did his all too soon passing. Gower born and Gower bred, he wouldn't have been surprised at all at the debacle that followed regarding the refusal by Pennard Community Council to allow his burial in the community graveyard: land that was once part of his father's farm at Kilvrough and given to the community for its residents. And that was the technicality that the committee ruled on, that Nigel was not officially of Pennard at the time of his death. This was a sad outcome for his family, Nigel could not go home. Nigel though, I'm sure, would have agreed that this was the stuff of Real Gower and it would have undoubtedly been expanded on in his psychogeography.

Nigel has now become part of the Gower earth he loved so much and shares the graveyard within the boundary walls of St Mary's Pennard with good company: the Swansea poet Harri Webb, who was a real influence on Nigel and another Gower bard Vernon Watkins. I think Nigel would like that.

Sometimes I believe you can love a place so much it becomes you, it permeates your soul like rain on limestone, like the snowdrops he loved to pick when they burst through the 'iron-fisted month' each year.

Gower seeped into Nigel's soul, coursed through his blood. And he will leave a lasting impression. Like an owl, swooping into his student's story:

> *The land is colourless, limestone grey, smudging impercep-*
> *tibly into the drained sky. Against this canvas, the owl sweeps*
> *and swoops at full span, its ivory plumage almost touchable*
> *it glides so close. It is the silence that is so shocking; such a*
> *big bird yet it is strangely noiseless for reasons I do not un-*
> *derstand. Other birds seem frenzied at this just before dusk*
> *time; but this white owl is serene, so calm. It circles above*
> *and then it does what I know it will – it comes to within yards*
> *of me, with its message. I read its eyes, startlingly bright in*
> *its flat, heart-shaped face. It connects for just long enough.*
> *And then it is gone into the long spring shadows.*

Recollections

Martyn Jenkins

Nigel and I had a lovely childhood growing up on a farm in Cilfrew, until we went away to school when we were about eight or nine years of age. There were so many special memories. We both had ponies but we had to ride them bareback unless father was present and then we could use a saddle – the reason being that if we did fall off we couldn't get caught and dragged in one of the stirrups.

We played cowboys and Indians, although both of us were cowboys there were always imaginary Indians present. I remember going to see a film about Davy Crockett who wore a big fur hat with a fox's brush tied to the back of it; he was a frontiersman, fighting the Indians and Nigel and I both bought a hat each, which we were very, very proud of. We also made our own farm in the woods, with a pretend cowshed and dairy and we had pots and pans which we washed like the real ones. Our tractors were old pram bases with wooden seats and the lawns were the fields where we spent many hours involved in imaginary ploughing and cutting hay and so on.

Nigel and I were both naughty boys but Nigel always stayed out of trouble unlike his brother who always got caught. Although we were both very close in age, Nigel always did things first, like partaking of alcohol, even though I soon followed. Unlike me he never smoked which was quite unbelievable really as all our friends smoked cigarettes at the time.

He passed his driving test before us and every Monday night we would go down to the Red Cliff, which was a hotel in those days, in Caswell Bay where a pint was two bob, or two and six for the very best, and we used to spend our wages there every Monday, and we had a lot of fun there with Paul Barry and Jeremy Smith. Those were special days, especially as Nigel was the main driver. He didn't drink and drive.

When we were away in Dean Close School we were about fifteen and sixteen he and a friend called John Atkinson bought a car, an Austen

Seven for a fiver and we used to keep it in the Lillybook Hotel outside Cheltenham at the bottom of Leckhampton Hill; the people who owned the hotel were very friendly with mum and dad. But they never let on that Nigel and John had the car. Nigel didn't have a licence or insurance yet he used to go out for a spin every Sunday. But the battery failed after a bit. Not being very mechanically minded they decided to pinch the battery off the school bus, a big old Bullnose Austen, not realising that the bus battery wouldn't fit in the car, the Austen Seven! So they pinched the battery off the car one evening, coming out of the dormitory and escaping into the night. The battery was so heavy that they had to drop it, abandoning it on a deserted railway line, somewhere between the school and the hotel. So the following Saturday they decided to enroll on the boating trip on the school bus, otherwise it would look a bit suspicious that they weren't on the trip, Anyway they got on the bus, which was completely dead and wouldn't start. So Nigel and the boys pushed it round the quadrangle and the old Colonel with a handlebar moustache said 'Some bloody bastard's stolen the battery!' That was typical of Nigel, he never got caught. He hated school. Every Monday they dressed us up as soldiers in the Army Cadets, with black boots. He absolutely hated that. We used to go to Gloucester Barracks to fire Bren guns and 303s but if you were really lazy you just went and put up the targets and you could smoke up there as there were no teachers up there, the noise was horrendous. We'd be putting up targets with live bullets coming over and then smoking and having a whale of a time.

On Sundays we used to go out on our bikes , with a so-called packed lunch, but we'd find a pub somewhere. He used to go to the corner shop and get an empty bottle and fill it full of cooking sherry and he and his pals would drink that. Terrible!

I remember us going to see the film *Ben Hur* with our mother and when we returned home – now being keen charioteers we got our ponies in from the fields and harnessed the old pram bases with baler cords (which were our tractors). Luckily our dad came home and averted the serious accident that would have certainly happened.

When we left school it was assumed that Nigel would go into the agricultural auctioneering business and I would be the farmer. In his teens he had become very interested in literature and had decided to go to university as he wished to become a journalist. Dad had wanted him to go into the business but accepted his decision.

I have spent my working life on Gower, well over forty years. When I left school in 1967, being an agricultural auctioneering valuer, I have had the privilege of visiting nearly every farm on the peninsula and many farms on the periphery of Gower. I've always enjoyed going to the various farms where the welcome has been very, very special.

After university he left home and took a job with the *Leamington Courier* in Warwickshire and therefore he never ever came back into the farming or the auctioneering business. Unfortunately I have no interest in poetry but I have enjoyed reading some of Nigel's poems relating to the family and books such as *Gwalia in Khasia*, the two *Real Swansea* books and the book about Gower with all the beautiful photographs.

In latter years I didn't see him as much as I would have liked to, because, thinking back, we were all doing our own things and time just passed us by. I suppose the last time we spent a lot of time together was the Gower show in 2005 when he returned to the show after missing it for forty years. He enjoyed that day.

Brother Nigel

Carey Knox

I was the 'baby' of the family and there was six years between Nigel and myself, and as kids I was classed as the 'baby' hence never really played with them; the two boys stuck together, as boys will be boys. As we grew up Nigel and Martyn were sent away to boarding school at the age of eight, and I remained home, and so, apart from holidays I hardly saw them.

When he was younger, Nigel was very conventional, but during his teen years that all began to change. He fought against the 'establishment'. He hated boarding school, and could not wait to escape, and left aged seventeen. He then went to Essex University while I was at boarding school, aged ten. I had little involvement with my two brothers.

Nigel loved to ride horses, as we all did, having been brought up on the farm, but our father was a traditionalist and while competing at a horse show, in his late teens, a lady asked my father who the young lady was riding his horse. It was Nigel, of course, with long hair in a pony tail. Dad was horrified that someone had called him a lady, and gave him an ultimatum: either have a hair cut or never ride again at a show. He chose the latter! It was a shame as he actually was a very good rider.

As a family – during holidays and on most weekends – we would all go for a ride together, usually to Three Cliffs and Pobbles, and sometimes to visit our parents friends across Gower. Without a doubt Gower was a huge part of our lives.

I remember riding with Nigel one day… as it happens it was at Pobbles, and he took off the saddle from his horse, and stripped to shorts, and rode the horse into the sea for a swim – he loved it! My father would have not been pleased had he known, as, to be honest, it was actually quite dangerous! But at the time we did not think of danger at all, just the exhilaration!

He'd ridden ponies and horses from before he could walk. One of my early memories was when Nigel and Martyn disappeared from the close vicinity of the house, and were very, very quiet. Mum and Dad wondered where they were, and more importantly what they were up to. They had tacked up their steady 'bomb proof' Welsh mountain pony 'Fairy', pulling them in a pram (mine) and were enacting the chariot racing scene from the film *Ben Hur*, tied to her bridle with two lengths of baler twine!

Nigel always was very good with words and also excellent in a debate; he would often completely overshadow the other participants. He used 'big' words, I had no idea what half of them meant at the time! He had a way with words and of course always spoke in that amazing, calm, beautiful tone and manner he became so well known for.

I never dreamt that he would become a writer. I always thought he would be a musician, he loved music: Bob Dylan, Joan Baez, Cream, Pink Floyd, Led Zeppelin, Eric Clapton to name a few. Music was always being played in his bedroom. He played the guitar and sung. In fact the boys, along with another friend who lived close by, formed their own band called 'The Urge'... they practised in one of the out-houses of the house, they were not good, but thought otherwise. Martyn was on drums, (certainly no Ringo Starr), Rod Thomas was a bass guitarist and Nigel on lead guitar and vocals. They never actually got any paying gigs. Come to think of it I don't think they got any free ones either.

I loved Nigel's 'humour poems'. I had two favourites: the drinking poem, 'Teetotalitarian Lament' which was read out at his funeral (although possibly not classed as a poem), and the alternative 'Welsh National Anthem'.

When I was sixteen I had a very bad horse-riding accident and broke my leg in two places. I had a plaster cast on from my toes to the top of my thigh, and had this on for six months. Nigel at this time lived in Leamington Spa working for the *Leamington Courier* newspaper, and writing, among other things, the entertainment pages, so had access to most venues/pop concerts. My mum lived at Stratford on Avon and I had gone there for a few weeks for a break. Nigel picked me up one day for a weekend stay with him, and took me to my first Pop concert, one the most amazing memories... I was so excited to see one of my favourite groups, Slade! I was taken back stage to meet the group. Noddy Holder, lead singer, and the remainder of the band signed my plaster... I thought I was the bees' knees being with my brother and with Slade!

He actually took me to see quite a few bands over the next few months, some heavy rock, not really my scene, but I had a great time. Having led quite a sheltered life I saw for the first time people taking drugs, this was totally alien to me! I hasten to add it was the band members and their 'groupies' on the drugs, not us!

Nigel did adore Gower. He spent any free time he had when younger riding around Gower, and in later years walking around Gower and writing about it. He was so proud of Gower and, I think, felt lucky to live in such a fabulous place.

He visited throughout his life so many countries as written in his books. He spent time in so many places, but always came home to Gower.

Sharing the Glee

Steve Dubé

'Fuck me to heaven in a bath of champagne', wrote Nigel in his 'An Execrably Tasteless Farewell to Viscount No'. He could smell gobshite at 100 paces and was a good shot with his pen. He didn't expect to find his photo and poem on the front page of *The Guardian*, but the death of the 'White man's Taff' and the 'Lord of Lickspit' – George Thomas – was 'a cowin' glee-bomb' for Nigel. Party friends of the 'smiley shyster' were suitably put out. The *Western Mail*'s letters page was replete with outraged apologists. But Nigel had told it like it was, sharing the glee around.

Another fond memory of a lovely man is the whole, and for us at the time, rare, bottle of brandy that sat in our sideboard for months until the Welsh Union of Writers committee meeting came to our home at Abernawmor, Pencader. Members had bought wine for the meal but this was gone by the end of the meeting, and before anyone was ready for bed. The brandy disappeared amid much merriment. The union was serious but fun, and the fun was serious. Alas, three of those who knocked back our brandy, John Morgan, Robin Reeves (who arrived brandishing a large double-handed hedge cutter from some job he was doing) and Nigel are now, I hope, raiding sideboards in another place.

It wasn't on this occasion that Nigel enjoyed his bath-time experience at Abernawmor. That must have been when we staged his play, *Strike a Light*, in the village, or when we hosted a performance by writers and musicians Nigel has befriended in Khasia. He and they stayed in the converted former cowshed we called the Hafod. Whatever the occasion, Nigel asked to have a bath, not even a bubble bath. Plain old hot water it may have been, but Nigel enjoyed plenty of it, and with vigour. Before long water began to drip, then pour through the floorboards into the living room below and I was dispatched upstairs to break the news.

We always enjoyed a laugh, whether we bumped into each other at a book launch when I was doing reviews for the *Western Mail* (the last time we met), at our homes; or on unique occasions like the unveiling of Gideon Petersen's great statue of Llywelyn ap Gruffydd Fychan in Llandovery when he read a poem and I piped a lament. He was someone you were always pleased to see.

It takes a brave man to chuck in the day job and choose to earn his keep in a Philistine world, from whatever he could scrounge from writing. But Nigel was brave as well as funny. Those four years as a young tyro reporter gave him skills he put to good use – shorthand, a concise use of English and a journalist's nose for human nature. He made it on his own where most of his contemporaries took comfort in some sort of nine-to-five. That independence gave him freedom and he found time, space and integrity to be a patron of the underdog and losing causes like CND and the aforesaid Welsh Writers' Union and, alongside Menna Elfyn and R.S. Thomas, the upstart effort in the late 1990s to win the franchise for a Welsh National Literature Promotion Agency to replace the Welsh Arts Council's literature department. Perhaps the bid was doomed from the start because of it was based in the more centrally located Newcastle Emlyn rather than Cardiff. The cheek! It caused a memorable stir among the Cardiff literati, who somehow engineered the failure of an impressive bid that would, among other things, have give Welsh lit a daily spot on Welsh radio. Makes you wonder, does that. Nigel, of course, harboured no grudges against the fixers and shakers of Cardiff. He was someone who knew that such things only weigh you down and slow you up. He could do without that. Now, alas, we have to do without him.

Tears of the Moon

Humberto Gatica

It was in the summer of 1985 when we met Nigel in Norfolk Street in Mount Pleasant, his first sentence was, 'Neruda changed my life'. He was talking about the Chilean poet Pablo Neruda, who not only changed the perception of poetry but, at the same time, showed the power of the language in the intensity of meaning when it is linked to the fact of history in the making. He was very surprised when I mentioned to him about the strong influence of Dylan Thomas in some of the Chilean poetry of the '50s.

'Sweat of the Sun/Tears of the Moon' was his idea for a bilingual reading of Latin-American poetry at Swansea University. With Nigel and the Chilean academic Luis Valenzuela, we spent many nights in the kitchen of my home discussing the selection of authors, poems and dealing with translations which ended with a selection of poems from Pablo Neruda, Ernesto Cardenal y Nicolas Guillen. The poem 'I Have' by Nicolas Guillen was included in Nigel's book *Hotel Gwales*.

The Poetry Workshop he was leading met in the Uplands. Part of the program was a selection of visiting poets, to read, discuss and answer questions about their writings with members of the group. He invited me to some of those meetings and I remember two names that were already known to me, Chris Torrance through his *Magic Door* and Peter Finch as the editor of *Second Aeon* magazine.

When *Planet* magazine decided to produce a Chilean Special issue, we were back in working meetings; Nigel was writing about the life of the Chilean community in exile and the musician Victor Jara. He wanted to verify some facts and tried to get deeper into the experiences and stories. I have a letter from that time in which he explains some events going on in the production of the issue and sent me the first issue of *Samizdat Wales*, which was produced very much in the style of the Russian underground publication, with poetry, ideas and debates about current affairs. His attitude to the Chilean cause at the time was not only of sympathy but a political compromise. He had a deep sense of social justice, human rights and freedom that put him in many fronts of struggles among others, his role in the Welsh Union of Writers and going to jail for refusing to pay the poll tax.

One Saturday at midday with Gabriela, my wife, we were in the city centre, when a long column of men in robes were approaching Castle Square. In the back was Nigel wearing a Druidic white robe.

He waved hello, smiled, then disappeared back into the group of wise men of mysterious and secret beliefs in the spiritual tradition of Wales.

Cowboys and Indians

An interview between Angharad Jenkins and Tom Jenkins

A.: Tom, who are you?

T.: Thomas Jenkins, Nigel Jenkins's nephew. He was my Uncle Nigel, my Dad's brother.

A.: How do you remember your Uncle Nigel? Was he very different from your Dad?

T.: They are very different. They're like polar opposites!

A.: In what way, then? In how they look?

T.: My Dad has short, back and sides, glasses and always wear a suit. And Uncle Nigel had long hair, beard, wore cowboy boots… always very casual.

A.: Were you ever, like, scared… cos lots of young people used to get scared of Dad. Cos he was so… like this... wild man.

T.: I don't think I ever was really. If you all came to the house, I'd always be quite sort of… I don't know the word for it…

A.: Sociable?

T.: Yeah I was… My brother wasn't. So I quite liked people coming to the house. So, yer know when your Dad used to come to the house when I came back from Portugal for a few Christmases, I'd always, yer know, come down stairs, and I looked forward to seeing him.

A.: So you weren't intimidated by him?

T.: No, not even as a youngster, I don't think I was.

A.: You said before that if you were talking he'd sort of…

T.: … Look at me, listen, and sort of, 'hmmm'. He wouldn't disagree with what I was saying, but he'd have this look. It could make you think 'have I said something wrong?'

A.: I think he was just listening.

T.: Or was he being polite!? I don't know.

A.: I think he was listening. He would be fascinated.

T.: He did always listen. I mean, he but always took a great interest in what ever I was talking about. And… obviously in my younger days, I used to talk a lot of rubbish! And he'd still listen, he'd still be interested.

A.: Tell me about that time, when every one came over to Dad's flat.

T.: About ten years ago, we came over for Sunday lunch. And we had beef with this gravy which was more like red wine – on its own! I don't think it went down very well with my father, who was good at cooking a roast himself. I think your Dad must have been sipping it and pouring it into the gravy at the same time. I know you get red wine gravy, but this was basically red wine. My Dad will remember it as well. It was dark red, with a tint of brown, and quite watery as well. But I think your Dad seemed to enjoy it.

So we had lunch, and then we drank quite a lot. Every one else went home, except for me. Me and your Dad wandered down to the White Rose, to finish the day off. And we just sat there then. We drunk pints of… I was drinking lager. I can't remember what he was drinking. I don't think he was drinking lager. I don't think he liked lager, did he? I dunno…

A.: He would drink lager. Maybe an ale, he might have been on...

T.: We had a good, yer know, we had a good few pints. And baring in mind we already had quite a lot with the red wine gravy, and all the drink in the house.

A.: So, he was a boozer?

T.: Well, I don't think it's for me to say really! But he liked a drink, yer know. He enjoyed a slurp or two.

A.: And at the time, you enjoyed a drink?

T.: Yeah, I was a bit of a boozer...

A.: In terms of what you were up to at this time. You were living in Swansea?

T.: At the time I was living in Swansea... I was quite off the rails I was. I was probably in the middle of my worst times. I was a cocaine addict and I had problems with alcohol. I had problems with all substances basically... all chemical substances. I was in the worst of my addiction at that time.

A.: Did Dad know that?

T.: Yes, every one did. It was common knowledge. But no one could stop me though. It was probably better not to say no to me.

A.: Why? How would you have reacted?

T.: Badly! I did once with your Dad. It says so in the letter. He came down the Joiners, I'd been there all day. And I'd had a skinful, and I think he'd had quite a few too. I wanted to go on to Mumbles, but he said no. He wouldn't give me a lift. I think I took it quite badly.

He would never have encouraged me to drink. Yer know, I never did drugs in front of him or any of the family. Every one knew about it, but I did that on my own. No, he didn't encourage me to drink. But that's what I did, I drank. So... And yer know, I didn't become a pain in the arse until later on in the nights, until I'd been on it all day, so, yeah... We just sat in the White Rose, and we talked about every thing.

A.: What would you talk about?

T.: My life... mainly about me. I think he was quite interested in... in... me, really. Whereas the rest of the family would sort of just shout at me. And, yer know. They told me I had to stop drinking, and stuff like this, whereas your Dad listened more. I don't know.

A.: He was probably also interested more in the 'other' side of Swansea.

T.: Very much so, I think. I was – as you know – very much involved in things in Swansea, I used to hang around in the more shadier places.

A.: This was probably before Dad started on the Real Swansea books, wasn't it? I suppose he never asked you to take him to these places.

T.: No. I'm sure, as I said, he did ask me in a letter that he'd like some input from me. But I don't know if I've still got that. But I think he was very interested in all aspects of Swansea, not just the nice parts. Yer, know, the shadier parts as well.

T.: When he sent these letters, I was in rehab in Bristol. Early 2005.

A.: Was this the first time in rehab?

T.: Yes, I think it was. No it can't have been my first time. Cos I've been... ten times. Jesus! But he still wrote to me, even though I messed up previous attempts.

A.: What about the rest of the family? Were they still speaking to you?

T.: Oh yeah, they spoke to me. But everyone told me what I had to do. And I mean in no uncertain terms, 'you've got to do this'. But he wasn't really like that. He wouldn't dictate to me what I had to do.

He was interested more than anything. And I think he understood that when people have problems such as I had, it's only that person who can turn it round. It doesn't matter what any one else says. I think he understood that. And he always showed an interest. He clearly didn't think anything worse of me, because I'd already been into rehab probably a few times before those letters. He knew that it was only me could do it, not any one else. He had much more of a calmer approach to it, I think. Which was better, really. I think, yer know, my auntie (my father's sister) possibly... she shouted at me. Whereas he had a calmer approach. And it was a better way about things really.

A.: And would you respond to him?

T.: I would respond to that. I wrote him letters back. And I can remember being straight with him as well, about my... yer know, various problems.

A.: In what way?

T.: I would be upfront with him. I could talk to him, and I could tell him the whole sentence, rather than having to cut bits out of it. Because I didn't mind him knowing. I suppose there was a little bit of trust. Because he was more laid back. That's what I meant. As I say, he didn't agree with it, but he was more sort of... calmer.

I was his brother's youngest son. But he had a different way about him than everyone else in the family. Well, he was completely different to everyone else in the family, wasn't he? He wasn't your typical Jenkins, I suppose. He wasn't straight laced. He'd often do his own thing.

A.: I don't know where he came from, he's so different! What does your Dad think of him?

T.: My Dad used to enjoy, and he'll tell you this. Every year your Dad would come over every Christmas to see us. My Dad could quite easily poke him. Cos they had different views. My father used to quite enjoy winding him up, I think.

A.: About what sort of things?

T.: About politics, the environment, current affairs. They had very different views.

A.: How were they so different, then? They were obviously very close in age, and went away to school.

T.: I think he'd rebel against authority. See… I was a bit like that. So I think that's where that comes from in me. I just took it to another level!

A.: So you've got a bit of Nigel Jenkins in you.

T.: Perhaps. Perhaps that's where the wild side comes from. One day I was in the Uplands Tavern… he was there and he was over the other side of the pub. I was with a load of my mates and we'd been out probably for days on end. So I was sort of fuelled up. And I'd got it in my mind that he ignored me. But he didn't ignore me, yer know… I don't think he saw me first of all. But I got it in my mind that he ignored me. And then I think I actually had a go at him. Not really nasty but, yer know, but 'Why did you fucking ignore me?'

A.: What did he say?

T.: Well, he didn't ignore me. He said, he didn't ignore me. It was in my mind, because I was so fuelled up with things. But I was a bit wound up, and I think he did calm me down. It was my fault again. But he never held that…yer know, he had friends there as well, but he never held that against me mind. I probably embarrassed him. Cos, yer know, I probably was a bit out of control. And he never held that against me.

But do you know what, I always remember for a few years after that, I always felt embarrassed about that. That time. Yer know, whenever he came round, that always entered my mind. And he never once said anything to me. Yer know, it was a done sort of thing.

He came over the house one day to pick up some manure. I don't know what it was for. But you know my father's got horses, hasn't he. So he came over to get some manure, or something.

A.: He didn't have a garden, but maybe... Margot used to have an allotment, so...

T.: Or was it some sawdust or something. I dunno. He went down the field with my father, and of course I had to go down with my dog. And I remember my dog jumping up all over her him! I don't think he was very happy! No, he didn't like dogs!

A.: He wasn't an animal person. Funny, because...

T.: He was bought up on a farm.

A.: He did have a way with horses. He knew how to deal with horses in a way, that I wouldn't...

T.: They used to play cowboys and Indians, didn't they? On horses, they used to ride... they used to tear around the field. I wonder who played the cowboy and who played the Indian?!

Nigel Jenkins
Top Flat
11 Chapel Street
Mumbles
Swansea SA3 4NH
WALES
01792-360685
01/02/05
n.jenkins@swansea.ac.uk

Dear Tom,

Had a chat with the old man last night, and he said you'd settled in to the Priory and that you were determined to make a go of it. Good for you, ten out of ten for intelligence, and congratulations on drumming up the courage to take this important – if not, indeed, life-saving – step. No one – least of all, I am sure, yourself – underestimates the nature of the challenge, but we are all rooting for you and looking forward to a healthier, happier Tom coming out the other side.

Your dad tells me that the Priory is like a posh hotel (without bar!), but, even so, I imagine it must feel pretty strange in the early days, as a stay in any new institution is bound to feel strange to start with. The people caring for you obviously realise this, and are no doubt doing their best to make you feel comfortable. I think back to my first days in certain institutions or situations: first week in work when I left home and became a reporter in the English Midlands; first week at university; first day of a year away when I went travelling for a year in mainland Europe and north Africa; first night – pitch black and with nowhere to stay – in Calcutta (that was a tough one, and how I missed the girls); and – the very worst of them all – first week in boarding school, aged 9. Some of these firsts were more welcome than others, even desirable in one or two cases, but all shared the same kind of strangeness, of not-belonging-ness, which eventually, of course changed into something more normal and easier to live through (apart from school, which I always hated and never grew to accept, and that was about an eight-year sentence – it still makes me angry). So I expect it will be a bit like that with you – feeling distinctly out of place to start with, but eventually finding your way around, making friends with new people and, as the treatment begins to work, enjoying the prospect of a future and looking forward to reconstructing your life. So hang on in there, gwboi, and stick with it. You've shown us you've got the courage to do this, and I know you've got the strength.

I rang the girls last night to tell them you'd arrived there safely, and they wanted to send you a text, but I told them mobiles were not allowed at the Priory (which, I suppose, makes good sense from various viewpoints). I've now got the landline number, so I expect they'll phone you soon – although you won't hear from Branwen, as she leaves today for Strasbourg, where she'll be staying for the rest of the week. I'll hand on your address to them too, so that they can write to you. Obviously, we'd all love to hear from you, but don't feel under any pressure to write – additional stress is the last thing you want at the moment. Only write if you get the time and feel like doing so. Do you have access to email there? That's far and away the easiest to make contact, I find. Worth having a go, even if you're not used to it. Dead easy to pick up the rudiments – if you can text, you can email, I should think.

way L ~~to~~ ∧

Not much news at this end. Last week I handed over to the publisher the finished *Encyclopaedia of Wales*, which was a great relief. It's been six years in the making, and it will be at least a year and a half more before it actually appears in the shops, because there is indexing and printing still to be done – but that is not my job, thank goodness. All that's left for me to do is tweak up the odd sentence when I notice in the press some new development in a situation, write a last-minute entry when someone notable dies, and read through the proofs. It's certainly been quite a tough job, with crazy hours (into the office by 7.00 a.m. and not leaving it, often, until 9 p.m.) and a difficult, frustrating management to work for, but the book itself is a good one, and I think it will do Wales some good.

So, as that project winds down, another looms: writing a 180-page book called *Real Swansea*, which, following the success of a book called *Real Cardiff*, written by a friend of mine called Peter Finch, is supposed to be an informal, personal view of Swansea, past and present – but particularly present. I will need to do a lot of research for this, which I will greatly enjoy. In fact, I am something of a research junkie, endlessly prolonging the research aspect of a job and endlessly deferring getting down to the actual writing. It will obviously involve a lot of reading – of books and archive material – but it will also involve a lot of tramping around, looking at things and talking to people. There are parts of Swansea I have never been, or hardly know – so it will be the perfect excuse for getting to know such places. I want to find out all sorts of things about 'hidden' Swansea. Where does our rubbish end up? Where are the sewers? What of the city's criminal life? Who's happy here? Who's sad? And on and on ... I'm really looking forward to getting stuck into this job, but first I have to agree a deadline with the publisher who, at the moment, is pushing me towards one which I can't accept. If I did, it would be replicating the pressures of Psycho, as we call our beloved encyclopaedic project. I want to talk to all sorts of people who know things that I don't know about Swansea – and would certainly welcome a long discussion or two with you, if you wouldn't mind sparing a bit of time in due course to talk about your Swansea and perhaps suggest places I should visit and take notes about.

Have got a huge amount of marking to do over the next couple of weeks, so I had better wind to a close now. As I think the girls may have mentioned to you, I wrote you a poem a while ago, which somehow didn't seem to reach you. Never mind; it's a bit out of date now, but the last line is still relevant: 'you owe your life its living' – which you do, Tom. You are beautiful, intelligent, of great charm, in good physical health (surprisingly, considering the hammering you've given your vitals over the last few years; I dread to think what my wine-enriched interior looks like) – and much loved. I expect that over the next few weeks we'll all be tossing ideas into the hat, to see if we can come up with ways of helping you to live that new life – and you can then pick and choose from them as to what may or may not be useful and appealing to you. Life should be good, Tom – and it will be, if you want it to be. You have all sorts of things going for you and everything to look forward to.

Let me know if there's anything (legal) I can send you, and give me a call (01792-295338 – office; 536718 – Margot's; 360685 – flat; 07984524969 – mobile) any time you like (I'll phone you back to save you money). Be happy and get well. We're all in there with you, in more ways than one.

With love,

Nigel

Nigel Jenkins

Tom Jenkins

Nigel Jenkins,
a gentleman, poet and a bit of a dude
With a fondness for beer, that was locally brewed
He was a man of stature who liked a good slurp
And if remembered correctly could produce a terrific burp!

The beard the hair and those cowboy boots,
Different to the rest, but stayed true to your roots
Our paths sometimes crossed and we'd drink pints with joy,
But would usually end up you saying, Thomas, time to go home
gwboi!

You listened with great interest to my stories of doom,
And would often reply with a nod of the head and a deep groan
of hmmm,
Thinking back I wrote you a poem which took me some time,
Then to my dismay you informed me it was just a rhyme!

I often think back and have a good laugh daily,
The lunch in your flat, with the dreaded red wine gravy!
Well it's time to end this beautiful poem of mine,
I know what your thinking,
It's not a poem gwboi, it's only a rhyme...

Doormen

David Hughes

We are in uniform:
white shirts, black ties.
Bulked up in overcoats
against the weather,
we stamp our feet,
suck mints,
reminisce,
waiting in the porch for his coffin.

The church full, we turn people away,
direct them elsewhere.

Bouncers at Nigel's last gig.

Arglwydd Dyma Fi

St Mary's Church Pennard

February 10th 2014

D.J. Britton

For Nigel Jenkins

We stand. The old song. The old tongue.
The ancient church, turreted against rain,
Against invasion, swells to our outward breath.
Sound carried on bass and treble,
And tones like stepping stones between.
We sing as one, in memory of one man.

The old song fills the dark places.
He the eternal man of here and I the visitor,
Bound by voices, sound sustained
By love and purpose and place.
The stone, the walls, the curved oak,
The public 'Our Father' on ancient painted boards.
No privacy of the pen here.

From the dark day beyond, a sun–flash jokes
Through sainted window glass, witty, irreverent;
And I hear his booming greeting in my own song,
As I did before in the pub or the office or his sitting room.
We hear it together. We are all here. We are all home.

Outside yellow soil oozes under shuffling feet.
He is home and he is gone.
I leave, a stranger still, but now a little less alone.

'Old Codgers Like Me' – the correspondence of Nigel Jenkins

Fflur Dafydd

I knew Nigel from an early age, as he was a close friend of my mother's. Every now and then, he came to stay with us to discuss translations of her poetry, and the very first thing I remember about him is finding his voice incredible to listen to. Like music itself. I have a distinct memory of lying in my teenage bed, trying to sleep, hearing booming, rich laughter reverberating through the floorboards, followed by whooping laugh of my mother, and the giggles of Iwan Llwyd. I had no idea at the time that the Nigel-laugh would work its way into my every day life, and would become the familiar, comforting chorus of my days.

Many years later, he became my colleague at Swansea University, and we formed a friendship of our own. He stopped being my mother's friend, and became not only my colleague but my mentor, inspirational not only as a writer but as an individual, one who could remain calm in all kinds of stressful situations, who could deal with any troublesome student, or any irate colleague, by rising gracefully above the mayhem, 'winking at the brim' of a coffee cup. When he later became Director of Creative Writing, I couldn't have asked for a more understanding or supportive boss; not that Nigel would ever be comfortable with being considered as a 'boss'. He had a certain way with bureaucracy. Dare I say he even found the poetry in it, finding lyricism in the illogical, delighting in rebelling against the drudgery, often without the 'system' knowing anything about it. Dutifully filling in forms, but always adding his own sardonic twist to the commentary, wondering whether anyone would notice. (And they never did.) He was the self-titled 'Fat Controller', trying to wade through what he called the 'impenetrable gobbledegook' of the system, never losing his patience or his humour.

His emails to me were like little life-rafts – aphorisms destined to keep me afloat, and his use of language was simply remarkable. I remember thinking that every correspondence from Nigel was frightfully, vibrantly alive, and I often marvelled at the creativity and wit of his articulation. I remember Professor Stevie Davies telling our new MA students how they had been 'listened to' in their emails before we had even met them, and that's certainly how I felt about Nigel's correspondence – his emails were ones I listened to. His emails were not just from him, they were him. Something sent from Nigel usually came back to me in little mnemonic waves, making me burst out laughing at the most inopportune moments, making me look like a madwoman, cackling into my sleeve. One such example was this email, sent after a particular gloomy academic meeting, in which we were encouraged to gather 'evidence' of our far-reaching 'impact' as writers:

> *I read to 500 people on Thursday, at the Inspire Wales Awards dinner, but I did not dish out questionnaires before-hand asking them to tell me that I had changed their lives. What madness. I don't think it matters much if old codgers like me can't be bothered with it all, but I can quite see that such exercises are important for members of staff of your generation. Good luck with it!*

Nigel was anything but an old codger, of course. He was as young as they come. A sprightly, young, dynamic, teacher – a comrade-in-arts, as he once wrote in a dedication, a visionary, in all sorts of ways. And always present, in an age of increasing business. Never making excuses for not being there. I can't think of a single event or launch where Nigel wasn't present – and he was committed, in particular, to encouraging emerging writers, those who were still finding their voice, and needed his support in order to feel valid, and, again, to feel as though they were being listened to.

He was simply adored by his students. Something interesting always happened in Nigel's class – there was hilarity, music, and near-nudity once! The rest of us could never compete. Every year, the students seemed to ask for more poetry, more Nigel. Right up until he became ill, he was inspiring people and introducing novice poets to new worlds. The reflective essays written by students following his death were difficult, but moving, to read. He had changed their lives; he had changed their vision. And that is a true gift, and a real legacy.

He was also a father, through and through. A father of daughters, which, in my experience, is a certain breed. Although he was a private person on so many levels, his daughters were a topic that was never off-limits, especially when I became a mother (of daughters) myself. I remember our countless conversations about Angharad and Branwen and how proud he was of them: 'the best thing I've ever done with my life' he once remarked, a curiously gushing comment from such an unsentimental man. The email I received from him following the birth of my daughter, Luned, a '10-pounder', still makes me laugh.

> *My goodness, that is one big baby. A mere man does not have the wherewithal to imagine how it must be to give birth to a baby, let alone one of those generous proportions.*

It is impossible to stress just how much we'll all miss him at Swansea University. And yet, it will only be a fraction of the loss that will be felt by those closest to him, and also the loss that will be felt in years to come, by the whole of Wales. We have lost a great poet and writer but also a great personality. Luckily for us, words are able to preserve a personality, and within his work we can still find that laugh, that warmth, that wit, that Nigelness, and that passion for life and for living – and it is a comfort to know that through reading him, we can still find him, and be close to him, time and time again. And with this in mind, I turn, yet again, to his words, and to his correspondence, for solace. He would want us to keep going. He would want us to look ahead, not back. For despite his occasional cynicism and dark humour, in Nigel's work there was always optimism. A planning ahead. That great impulse to move forward. And the endless hope of reaching calmer shores, be it figuratively or literally. And so perhaps it is apt to end with his hopeful words, to bring us back towards the light:

> *Things are looking up after a gloomy September, it seems: we now have an Indian summer to look forward to. The swimming season is not yet over!*

The Naming of Things

Anne Lauppe-Dunbar

Nigel was that rare friend you might meet along the cycle track that takes you from Mumbles to Swansea, or after a swim in the icy waters where 'at the eastern end of the promenade is the delightful cove of Rotherslade…'[1] We met once, at this 'delightful cove'[2] purely by chance. I, clumsy-mouthed and awkward, my sandy towel wrapped around a goose-bumped cossie as I scrambled to find trousers, top, – professionalism? I had trundled down Rotherslade hill barefoot, having moved to a small back apartment in the house that used to be a hotel called Bryn Teg, on the corner where Higher Lane meets Overland Road.

> Wheeling from silver water to stone crag
> I find – pure joy.
> The tide is turning,
> swirling foam eddying over my feet.[3]

Nigel, already dressed in comfortable trousers and a large t-shirt, asked if I'd like a coffee. Me? Coffee? Nigel? This man was a poet, a wordsmith whose rumble of perfect Welsh *iaith* tumbled from his mouth. A rumble we so loved to hear. I muttered a muted 'Love to', and moments later we were stood by the 'Rother's Tor Café, with its broad terrace for tables and chairs'[4] now known as Surfside Café @Rotherslade. I realised I hadn't brought any money, and was about to say so, but Nigel had already disappeared into the gloom of the café to emerge some moments later with two cappuccinos.

Virginia Woolf writes in her autobiography *A Sketch of the Past*: 'If life has a base on which it stands upon, if it is a bowl that one fills and fills and fills – then my bowl without a doubt stands on this memory.[5]

I remember this moment, a defining vignette: the heat of the lumpen concrete terrace under my heels, the deep late afternoon sun, a hugeness of sand and sea and sky reflected in my joy at simply being here. An overheated

Scottie dog panted a hot, salty longing for that last drip of strawberry ice cream that was pinking its way round and round a child's rosy arm.

'Mam,' pleaded a small boy in green plastic shoes that squeaked, 'carry – up, up.'

I remember thinking – what was I to say to this poet? Talk about the weather? Work? My idiotic attempts at poetry? I scowled into my coffee and felt, as I often do, completely out of my depth. How could I, the mad girl who ran away from school, home and all possibility of hope, have a conversation with a bard? Nigel, happy in his world, spoke about the sea. Now, he said, was the best time to swim as the sand had warmed, and the crowds had dissipated. He disarmed then humbled me with his kindness. Rather than reaching for a rhetoric I could only dream of, he leaned towards the warmed earth of his beloved Gower and patiently showed me how to pronounce Pwlldu, wincing only very slightly as I said 'Pulldoo', hissing and squelching my mouth around the 'hrcch' as any German speaker might. We spoke of the how the light traversed the grey ocean. How '"old timers' whose habitual domain – for reading, talking, eating and drinking – is a sun trap in the cove's eastern corner.'[6]

He revealed how he and Stevie Davies competed over the summer to see how many times each would swim. I thought (oh, fool that I am) I could beat them, but never got anywhere near, even though, in 2013, I tried to convince Nigel that diving counted for at least ten Rotherslade swims, and since I'd dived six times, each time an hour, well, that counted for… sixty swims?

'Not a chance,' he said.

My pronunciation of places, beaches, street names remained a challenge. When I moved to Folland Court, West Cross, I avoided getting the bus from work for fear of being seen as a complete imbecile.

'Nigel, how might I pronounce Llwynderw Drive?'

That wince, fleeting as the coffee-at-at-Rotherslade-day, was again replaced by kindness as he patiently showed me how to get it right. The bus driver was less forgiving.

'What you on about pet? Llynderooo?' *Pet*?

Nigel's use of language, his poetry, is serious – as it is fun, grounded, in flight, gentle as dew, precise – as perfect as any I have known. He was a man of the sea and the sky, yet so rooted in the damp earth of Gower he became part of the landscape, part of my landscape. I would catch him cycling to work as I cycled home. He helped me see that we all have feet of clay even if, or when, we might fly for a brief moment. I never felt stupid in his company.

Along with Margot's choir, we entertained the great master of words over handmade mince pies and mulled wine – the winter of 2010. I wrote of it in my diary: 'Cat on table cleaning its right paw as we sing "He's the Lily, of the Valley". And so he is.'

Whenever I could I joined the group of new MA students he would take on a walking tour, showing them a glimpse of real Swansea. He named each street, the old buildings and where they stood, the new, the places that had been and would be again, though in a different form. Tired, we would end our walk at Wind Street and the No Sign Bar with its

> 'traditional' ambience – bare wooden floor floors, reclaimed furniture, 'distressed' paintwork, glass cabinets, fireplaces, old bottles on dusty shelves, and no alcopops, no robotic dance music ... makes it warmly welcoming of 'old' (those treasurable inverted commas) people like me (and younger ones too) who enjoy a chat or a read in congenial surroundings.[7]

Here, we'd eat and drink and regale one another with our stories.

The idea that 'places also take on aspects of their names, at least if they touch something to begin with'[8] is something Nigel believed. He spoke of names as if they evoked meaning:

> Gowerton has had several names. It's first, naming a junction of farmers' and drovers' tracks near todays' Welcome to Gower pub, was Ffosfelin (ditch + mill) after a cornmill built near Llan in 1680 and demolished in 1939 (one of the millstones is on display outside the library in Mansel Street). That much of the surrounding land was no more than a boggy morass has suggested to some that the hamlet's original name was Ffosfelen (yellow ditch).[9]

He was intrinsically linked to the place in which he lived. A true part of its history in that his family' who, as well as being farmers, had run the [Gowerton] mart for generations.'[10] I wondered at his ability to truly belong, to be part of his landscape. I had never sensed 'an aching *Hiraeth*'[11] until I walked the streets of my ancestral home in former East Germany and felt a perplexing longing for something I couldn't explain. Perhaps I was feeling a sense of *Heimatland*: the sense of a home (or a home-land). Not so much a specific place, as a feeling.

In William Moon's book *PrairyErth*, the writer goes further to uncover, as does Nigel, the complexity of a name and its meaning:

> *I've come across 140 ways to spell Kansas, and, if you in-clude the confused Ac-, Es-, Ex-, Ok-, Uk- forms at times ap-plied to the tribe, I've found 171 variations that employ every letter of the alphabet except b, f, and v. The question comes up, if whites couldn't get a three- or six-letter word correct, what else couldn't they get right? The meaning of the word for one thing: Kansa and its forms have been translated as wind, windy, wind people, south wind people, those-who-come-like-the-wind-across-the-prairie, swift, swift wind, swift river, swift water, smoky water, fire people, plum peo-ple, disturbers, troublemakers, filthy and cowards. Dispense with the freak translations like the last four, and you have a people defined by three of the four ancient elements.*[12]

Nigel's attention to naming, to place, to detail, was a wonderful thing. His joy in the moment: rooks making their daily circle; not dissimilar to The Wave at a sports match, outside his office window, was matched by a keen historical knowledge. He knew that 'Swansea was originally a Celtic settlement known as Senghenydd (Sein + Henyd (d)), after one of Wales's two saints Cenydd'[13] and that 'it may therefore also have been known as Llangenydd (or Llangeneu or Llanngemei or Lan Gemie: the church of Cenydd, Morgan maintained, stood where the Normans later built their castle').[14] Nigel knew stuff. Stuff I could only gawp at and try, with his help, to pronounce. He had a map of Swansea and Mumbles on his office wall. I have my own now, emblazoned across the sitting room wall so that I can peer and squint at street names. Try them out, try again, and perhaps, occasionally, get the sound right.

'If I were a painter', Virginia Woolf writes. 'I should paint these first impressions on pale yellow, silver, and green.'[15] Nigel spoke of his rambles in Gower as glorious impressions of colour, story, and history, of mud, sun, and thick rain. There is the loveliness of Rotherslade where local swimmers are defined as blue scribbles on the far horizon; sand stretches round like the perfect half of a vanilla ice cream cone: one scoop, not two. Swansea, and that moment of sunset where the windows blink their nightly Morse code, Mumbles, Brandy Cove and Pwlldu, where, today, the wooded path from Bishopston is awash with late bluebells and sweet wild garlic.

I like to think of him striding across fields and brooks, peering into the burgeoning hedgerow, naming each hamlet, each church, each plaque; bearing out a history of what was and what is now.

Notes:

1 N. Jenkins, *Real Swansea* (Seren Books, 2008), p. 173.

2 Ibid, p. 137.

3 A. Lauppe-Dunbar, *Caswell Bay* (2006).

4 Ibid, p. 176.

5 V. Woolf, *Moments of Being* (Pimlico, 2002), p. 78.

6 N. Jenkins, *Real Swansea* (Seren Books, 2008), p. 177.

7 Ibid, p. 104.

8 W. Moon, *PrairyErth* (Mariner Books, 1999), p. 118.

9 N. Jenkins, *Real Swansea* (Seren Books, 2002), p. 178.

10 Ibid, p. 178.

11 N. Jenkins, *Real Swansea* (Seren Books, 2002), p. 19.

12 W. Moon, *PrairyErth* (Mariner Books, 1999), p. 120.

13 N. Jenkins, *Real Swansea* (Seren Books, 2002), p. 16

14 N. Jenkins, *Real Swansea* (Seren Books, 2008), p. 16.

15 V. Woolf, *Moments of Being* (Pimlico, 2002), p. 79.

Dad Part 2

Angharad Jenkins

To many, Nigel Jenkins was the cowboy-boot wearing Welsh poet, but to me he was about the cut off jeans, leather sandals and the charity shop shirts from Tenovus, his 'local tailor'.

Summers with Dad were all about the 'Barbies down *Rothers'*. (Rotherslade – but Dad would often enjoy abbreviating words.)

The BBQ was a stumpy chrome cylinder, with a handle on the top for ease of transport, and four feet on the bottom for well-balanced cooking, whatever the surface. The cylinder was held together with a latch, and when unclipped, the cylinder would fall into a double grill, perfect for cooking up a feast.

Our favourite patch at Rothers was hidden away amongst the rocks to the left of the beach as you looked out to the sea. We'd climb up through a gap in the rocks near the top of the beach just where the pebbles end and the fluffy sand starts, and then turn right through a natural passage between the rocks. Our patch was a sun drenched concrete platform, with enough shelter from the surrounding rocks to light the old Barbie. It was a fairly ugly bit of concrete, but from the platform we had a perfect view of the whole of Rotherslade, right along to Langland, and we could watch the tide as it came in and out.

Once we'd set up camp, the first task was to light the Barbie, before stripping down to our bathers for a dip in the sea. Dad would have to pull out his contact lenses first. He would kneel down, and throw a towel over his head to block out any stray grains of sand. He'd gently rub his right index finger along the tip of his tongue, before scooping a lens from each eye and placing them in their white and blue plastic container.

With Dad's wrist watch safely left in a pile of clothes on the rocks, we'd loose all track of time in the sea. It would be a competition amongst us as to who would go for the 'full-emersion' first. When it came to 'full-emersion' Dad was usually a lot braver than Branwen and me, and he would kindly help us along with a whopping great windmill splash – stretching his arm out and skimming the surface of the water to create a human wave, substantial enough to drench us so much that we'd surrender to the cold sea. With a gasp of breath, and a panicked doggy paddle, we'd soon acclimatise to the temperature.

We'd stay in the sea until the skin of our fingers and toes shriveled in the cold salt water. We'd play lots of games in the water together. Dad would swim through our legs, we'd swim through his. There would be hand-stands, and pale white legs kicking the air. We'd sit on Dad's shoulders, and he could even sit on ours with the help of the sea's buoyance. Sometimes Dad would disappear under the water, and pop up like a seal, a few moments later somewhere totally unexpected. When the sea was calm Dad would float on his back enjoying the tranquility and peace, the faint chatter and laughter of the beach-goers on the shore in the distance. 'Aren't we lucky,' he'd say, 'to live in such a beautiful place.' But when the sea was rough, it was time for body surfing! He taught us how to wait for the wave, and at the perfect moment, start swimming ahead of the wave before it would catch us and whisk us away to the shore with it. At its roughest, the sea would carry us right to the shore until our bellies would scrape along the sand. A dizzying pause, a moment of stillness to get back on our feet, and then a cry of delight. Yes, we did it! Before heading back into the sea. Dad was a water baby, and these were very happy days.

After fun and games in the sea, we'd return to the Barbie, which would by now be perfectly heated, and ready for the meat. There would be burgers, *selsig*, corn on the cob, minted lamb from the butchers. There would be fresh bread, potato salad, bean salad, and to drink *dŵr* or *sudd afal*. We'd often go for a *hufen-iâ* from the café in Rothers or Langland, but as we got older something a little more exciting was added to the menu, in the form of an aluminium tumbler of Rioja, or perhaps a bottle of OSB.

Yes, Dad taught me how to drink. 'You've got a constitution like your father', Mum would go on. But that's for another time.

I remember one time as the day was drawing to an end we were enjoying ourselves so much on our platform that we hadn't noticed the tide come in. We gathered our stuff together, and headed back along the rocky passageway to the beach. By this time the tide had come in so far it had created a deep rock pool along our route back to the beach. Branwen and I were able to avoid the rock pool and jump nimbly on to a rock which was only submerged under about a foot of sea water. The rocks were slippery so we were deep in concentration when we heard a giant splash. We turned round, and all we could see of Dad was his face and shoulders above the water and his arms, holding up our beloved BBQ and protecting it from the sea. We all burst out laughing, and helped him out of the rock pool. And then we had to do the walk of shame along the beach back home. Dad with a clear line along his chest, his bottom half was darker from the sea water. If you've ever seen the Vicar of Dibley when Dawn French jumps into a muddy pool and ends up to her neck in mud, then this was the rock pool equivalent!

Our other favourite beach was Slade. Again, this beach wasn't the easiest to reach.

Dad took us to some extraordinary places.

I suppose, because he left when we were teenagers, our time with him was so precious, and we were to make the most of it. We'd go to stay with him every weekend, and go for tea after school twice a week. Tea times were a big thing, and he'd always cook up a feast. Curry, salmon and prawn sauce, tarragon chicken… these were some of the favourites. Followed almost always by fruit salad and Joe's ice cream. Some times we'd walk along the front to Verdi's for an after-dinner coffee, or nip along to Castle News to pick up a bar of Lindt chocolate. Dad had a weakness for chocolate.

Tea times were also about spontaneous music making. Using cutlery as beaters, we'd tap glasses and plates, and run knives along the springs on the angle poise lamp, flexing the lamp forward and backward to change the tone of the twang. It was at tea times hits like 'It's a Limousine' and 'In Abergavenny' were written.

The time would come to catch the 2A bus back home to Caswell, or sometimes mum would pick us up. Dad would be left alone, to write.

The Real Thing

M. Wynn Thomas

My friend and colleague Nigel Jenkins now lies – unbelievably – in Pennard Churchyard, in his native, and beloved Gower. I pass the spot ever day and never fail to put in a good word for Nigel to the Almighty, in whom he did not believe.

The department is so quiet without him. 'I so miss the laughter that came from Nigel's room', a colleague told me the other day. That laughter always came from some colleague or other who had been the latest recipient of Nigel's acidly witty comments on the asinine culture of modern universities governed by apparatchiks and bureaucrats.

He never missed an opportunity to sabotage the system. 'Stevie Davies is a wondrous teacher', he wrote on one peer review form. 'She leaves her students swooning with delight and prostrate with admiration.' 'I am deeply offended,' he wrote on a self-assessment form, 'at the number of people in this university who walk the corridors with their sleeves rolled up. It disrespects the dignity of this esteemed academic institution. Gowns would be preferable, but failing that shirt sleeves should, at the very least, be firmly buttoned at the wrist.'

'The buggers never read these forms anyway', he used to tell his colleagues as he sent his forms off to HQ.

All this is by way of saying that Nigel, unlike so many others in university life these days, it seems to me, was the real thing. He was a splendid poet, a scholar whose *Encyclopaedia of Wales* – which was his encyclopaedia, although he ostensibly 'only edited' it – is one of the great modern monuments of Welsh history and culture. He was an incomparable teacher of creative writing, genuinely adored by his students. He was a passionate and deeply informed lover of Wales, and an equally impassioned progressive internationalist. He was an accomplished journalist, a superb organiser, an astute cultural commentator, a fine and original cultural historian, a courageous campaigner… and the list could be considerably extended.

My colleague, Daniel Williams, captured some of the essence of Nigel when he wrote that he railed incessantly 'against the vultures of unthink,' but could also 'conjure dreams of buccaneering bohemian restlessness on the one hand, or a deep meditative rootedness on the other'. Daniel recalled, as so many of us of a certain generation do, Nigel's outspoken lampoon of the recently deceased George Thomas MP, Speaker of the House of Commons, whom he described as 'the Lord of Lickspit,/ The grovelsome brown-snout and smiley shyster', 'Queen-cwtshing Brit Nat.' It's as if a Gerald Scarfe cartoon had suddenly started to speak.

As an unsparing satirist, Nigel had a sensitive crap-detector. But he was also a fine love-poet. A splendid poet of local place, he also wrote a poetry of cosmic reach and vision. A free spirit, he somehow seemed most at home on his bike, self-propelled, independent, unconfined, comrade of wind and weather; in his element, in more senses than one, having been born and raised after all on a farm.

Had there been a competition to discover the sexiest voice in Wales – an eisteddfod competition, say, adjudicated by Tom Jones – then Nigel would have won it hands down. No one, therefore, will ever be able to read his poems off the page in his own incomparable way. But he ensured that those poems of his do have in them life more than enough to speak for themselves, and so they are sure to live on in readers' hearts and minds for generations yet to come.

A Tutelary Spirit

Jon Gower

He taught me stuff, did Nigel.

He taught me, in one of his sharp and sassy triads, that the brewery horse at Welsh Brewers must have diabetes, judging from the piss they served. He taught me that it is possible to love a place so much that it becomes you. And he showed me, effortlessly and in so, well, gentlemanly a manner, how to live in a spirit of selflessness and complete generosity. That generosity was seemingly embodied in that voice of his. If ever a pint of Guinness had a voice then it would be Nigel's. Dark, velveteen, nourishing and deep. Resonant as ocean's undertow. But it was there in the writing, too, in great measure. A generous respect for others, manifested by being deeply interested in other folk and their various ways. But no respect for bull-shitters, lickspittles, establishment toadies. He had his demarcations. And they were very, very clear. Lines in the sand. Lines you dare not cross. Not if you were a bureaucrat, that detested breed. Or a fan of the Royal family. Or someone who wanted to be a poet simply for the glory and the prizes of it.

Nigel was such a giving man. Good will, support for others, excellent karma, the deepest kind of wisdom and a ready wit flowed from him. He gave in person, or over a pint of (proper) beer or a glass of his beloved Rioja, in e-mails that seemed as carefully worked as old-fashioned letters, via his Stakhanovite work on 'Cyclops,' or 'Psycho' – being, in common purlance, the *Welsh Academy Encyclopedia of Wales* – and through his books, which were always gifts, they truly were.

Somewhat egotistically I thought that I was somehow special, that Nigel had singled me out for extra care and attention. After his death it became only too clear that he gave extra care and attention to legions of people, to pretty much everyone in range, and certainly to all his students. If we managed to pull all of his letters and e-mails together, then bound them carefully as solid books in skins of leather, they'd be at least as substantial as those compendious complete works of the Albanian leader Enver Hoxha that you used to see, unloved and unsold in secondhand bookshops. But Nigel's letters, well, they'd be giving love, and wisdom and insight. Gather them while we can! Now there's a proper, rewarding task for an academic researcher.

If you yourself are lucky enough to have some of these letters, consider how much time went into even a routine e-mail. He always gave you a little bit extra, a nugget of information, a quantum of support, an acid *bon mot* about the bureaucracy that weighed him down like a overcoat made of granite.

In so many ways Nigel taught me how to write. I once took an MA class for him and asked him what he normally took as his subject in that week. He explained, with a touch of typical diffidence, that he normally used his own *Gwalia in Khasia*, but stressed that I could base my workshop on any book I liked. I remember how pleased he was when I said that I'd teach *Gwalia* too, and do so without notes, as I knew it so well. I doubt if I was ever his peer, but this sort of peer-respect was the best way I could underline my regard for his impeccably researched book. The fact that I'm currently writing a book called 'Gwalia Patagonia', modeled on, and inspired by Nigel's Book-of-the-Year-winning account of the Welsh in the Khasi hills, serves only to underline his very real and abiding influence. I've read it three and a half times and plan to read the remaining half just as soon as I've finished writing this piece. *Gwalia in Khasia* is that sort of book. A genuinely compelling read, even from the very first sentences:

> *The Khasis compute their history with stone. Across the hills and lost plains, in their jungle villages and even on the streets of their car-choked capital, long shadows fall from countless thousands of cromlechs and monoliths. Remember, they say, the mother of mothers, remember the dead and venerate their deeds; remember what has been sworn on the blades of swords. The very word for 'remember', kynmaw, is megalithic: 'to mark with a stone'.*

The book is pretty megalithic, solid with journalistic and historical research, but never heavy going. *Gwalia in Khasia: a visit to the site in India, of the biggest overseas venture ever sustained by the Welsh* is a masterwork of travel writing, which properly places Nigel Jenkins up there in the pantheon alongside such well travelled luminaries as Rebecca Solnit, Bruce Chatwin, Patrick Leigh Fermor, Jonathan Raban and Paul Theroux. Not that he wrote much else in the travel writing line. His writer's or writerly journey was to grow increasingly concerned with home, with Wales and Swansea and Gower. But with Khasia he found his grand canvas, on which he could daub and illustrate a dizzy mix of adventure and cultural examination, all benefitting from his journalist's attention to detail and poet's tool kit for spelling it out, able to find the sublime in the mundane when necessary. There are pointillist passages, Old Master flourishes, quiet etchings and deep engravings, all within the space of a few pages.

He was lucky, of course, to discover such a great story, and one with such deep Welsh connections. Funded by a John Morgan Writing Award, some TV money and a subvention from his mother Gloria, the book tells the fabulous and largely forgotten story of the Welsh Calvinistic Methodists' Mission to the Khasi Hills of north-east India between 1841 and 1969. If the main intention was to convert local souls to Christianity then the figures speak for themselves, or pretty much sing a hymn to success, with no fewer than 300,000 Khasis turning Presbyterian. There were side-benefits too, in terms of literacy and literature, the establishment of school and hospitals, a veritable transformation of the material as well as the spiritual culture. But this did not come without its cost, as acts of colonizing are seldom innocent or benign. Nigel doesn't don rose-tinted spectacles when he looks at such matters, but rather fixes things with a gimlet gaze. He wants truth, nothing less, while being also uncommonly alert to beauty, even as he charts the tawny hills very much with a moral compass. These people didn't choose the hymns: they were foisted upon them. Missionary work was seldom benign, even if the intentions were Christian and good.

This is the book that introduced me to the writing tool that is the list. At one point in the story Nigel gives us a two-page account of the

naming of Khasi children, whose parents like, above all else, names that
are euphonious, even though there are those parents who choose names
loaded with promise such as Barrister, Wordsworth, Hamlet or Pascal.
But it's the names that rhyme and chime that often win out:

> *Khasi siblings often rhyme and alliterate: Karen and Sharon;*
> *Sufficiency and Efficiency; Edify and Modify – known to*
> *their pals, of course, as Edi and Modi.*
>
> *But there must have been those, entranced by the sound of*
> *a word, would have chosen differently had they known at the*
> *time precisely what it meant – the parents, for instance of U*
> *Atom Bomb, who must have fallen for those eerily mantric*
> *words having heard them on the radio soon after August 6,*
> *1945; or the parents who christened their lovely daughters*
> *Toilet and (no relation) Latrine. They could have done worse,*
> *I suppose, like the Shillong woman who was named Prosti-*
> *tute, Kong Pro for short.*
>
> *But three cheers for the garage mechanic who, having had*
> *two boys, Piston Rod and Crankshaft, desperately wanted a*
> *daughter. At last his wife gave birth to a girl, and he chris-*
> *tened her Mobil Oil.*

He was many things and had many gifts, but I'd like to home in on
the psycho-geographer, not least because we both wrote books in the
'Real' series of books, helmed by the irrepressible Peter Finch. Nigel's
Real Swansea came out in 2008, just as I was researching the equivalent
tome about Llanelli. His book weighed in at 222 pages and so, egged
on by the old, old rivalry between Llanelli and Swansea, between the
Turks and the Jacks I told him that Real Llanelli would be bigger, as
there was so much more to say. And so it transpired with my book being
slightly more substantial, despite my home town being smaller, and
certainly not a city. Nigel appreciated the joke, and even came to the
lion's den to discuss the relative merits and demerits of both places when
we staged an event at the Llanelli Entertainment Centre. But then he
trumped me, fair and square, by responding with the successor volume

Real Swansea Two at 264 pages! I told him I was working on *Real Llanelli 5* but my bluff was well and truly called. The two books (not to mention the forthcoming volume about *Real Gower*) form a magisterial and engaging account of his adoptive city, which put some ozone into his lungs as the wind swept in from open ocean and inspired love for its streets and history, industrial past and anticipated future. Living and working in what might be described as Wales's second city (not a term of disrespect as so many of the world's second cities are, in fact the cultured ones) – engaged that boundless, youthful, Jenkins' curiosity. The place allowed him to celebrate – in that meticulous, measured and often downright bloody marvellous prose of his – just how such a place could prove the truth in Vernon Watkins' assertion that 'Prouder cities rise through the haze of time/ Yet, unenvious, all men had found is here.' And with this book, as with his others, Nigel argues his place in the Swansea pantheon.

So am I talking him up because he was a friend? I don't think so. He's one of those writers I've read and re-read – others who get the same treatment include Robert Minhinnick's essays, Marquez's short stories, Updike's everything – and he always reveals something new, something freshly peeled back and exposed. It's not just the writing, though, it's the politics that chimes, the Republicanism coupled with Internationalism – big, though increasingly unfashionable ideas (or maybe it's just all political thought that's been dismissed, seen by many as desiccated, or corrupt, or both) which I still find conducive to the patriotic loving of a country. This country. Wales. And Nigel loved the land as well as its people, able to regale us with accounts of humanized landscapes – or, in the case of Swansea in its metallurgical heyday – a de-humanizing landscape, under a skein of sulphurous smog and through which the Tawe ran pretty much hydrochlorically.

In the first volume Nigel penned about Swansea he manages to bring the whole city to life just as surely as the TV drama 'The Wire' conjures up Baltimore, or Saul Bellow brings Chicago to pulsing life, or Peter Ackroyd gives us London. It sometimes takes a writer to properly put a city on the map, or simply, to make us believe it fully and truly exists. So, just as Paris needed Proust, or Dublin its Joyce,

Buenos Aires its Borges, so too did Swansea need its writers. And Nigel understood it better than any of them, Dylan Thomas and Vernon Watkins included. He walked Constitution Hill so many times he had, surely, the calf muscles of a Bhutanese Sherpa. He drank in the atmosphere – or simply drank in – the city's cornucopia of pubs, from the Queens to the White Rose, not forgetting the paradisical Adam & Eve, now closed, the final stop tap. His annual city ramble for new students in the Creative Writing Department were an open air master class in short cuts, accessible history and the delights of the place. Real Swansea is, perhaps, the unabridged version of those guided tours, taking in the sights. I mean really taking in the sights:

> *If you stand at Mumbles when the tide's in, with perhaps a rowing team slicing over the bay's glassy surface, and a dozen mute swans tacking and preening on an almost imperceptible swell, there being no sign in this apparently landbound scene of any egress to the Severn Sea.*

> tide in, skiers out
> – dollar signs carved
> from shore to shore

From the Zen, millpond stillness of the sea off Mumbles the book takes us pretty much everywhere, from the new sewage treatment plant at the Green Grounds in 'a city by the sea that seems not to care a seagull's fart about being by the sea' through the 'marine vernacular' of the new bay-side flats and developments, to the shiny express or espresso way of the SA1 development. Along the way we get the history of the great musician Spencer 'Keep On Runnin'' and 'Gimme Some Lovin' Davis and explore the origins, and, indeed, the tale of Swansea Jack. We see the last flickering memories of the old cinemas, climb up the Uplands, climb even higher up Kilvey Hill, a fine vantage point from which Jenkins can ponder the reclaiming of the blasted, lunar and totally toxic landscape that was the Lower Swansea Valley, with its 'huge boulders of fused slag, mounds of multi-coloured toxic waste, crumbling smokestacks, decaying smelter sheds and abandoned sidings'. It's not an easy climb at any time, is Kilvey, but Nigel, when he attains the summit spares a thought for those unfortunates who take part in the annual Kilvey Hill Cement Run which involves running a mile up the hill with a 50kg bag of cement on your shoulders. Bonkers, yes, but all in a good cause and it's a telling detail, the sort of thing which lifts the material, gives it spark and life and a whiff of eccentricity. The book is peppered with such asides and telling facts, about anything from the spread of buddleia to the history of the dockland glory days, when Swansea sent out the world's copper, bringing back Chilean guano and tall tales galore. I hope I told Nigel about the sailors' habit of painting picture postcard type scenes of the places they visited on to a single bird's feather and posting that back to their loved ones in Swansea. But, then again, he probably knew this anyway. His was a capacious memory, buoyed up by an inquisitive love for the city.

There's a small, domestic tale in *Gwalia in Khasia* that stays in the mind. Nigel has been taken by a poet friend of his, Desmond Kharmawphlang to visit a village storyteller. His story, when it's finally told, concerns the Sun, the Moon and a Hornbill, but it's not the story itself that stays in the mind but, rather the preparations made for telling it and Nigel's own appraisal of the poetry that flows from the old man's desiccated lips:

> *There is a ritual to be observed. First his daughter, slim and sassy with her broken-toothed smile, wraps a turban round his head which she has woven herself. Then, squatting on a stool in the middle of the yard, he places on the ground in front of him the traditional egg-breaking board, the* dieng shat pylleng; *alongside it he puts a metal cup full of water and a small basket containing rice and an egg. He slops some water over the black wood of the board to clean it, then deposits some rice at its centre and a pinch of five or six grains at each corner.*
>
> *Chanting, he places the egg on the nest of rice in the middle of the* dieng. *Then he picks it up, spits on it, rolls it round*

in his hand and launches into the story, his voice rising and
falling as if in the throes of some oriental blues. He is clearly
in a trance, oblivious to what is going on around him.
'This is truly marvellous,' whispers Desmond. 'The flow of
his language is beautiful – he's saying things now that he
would never be able to say in normal everyday circum-
stances.'

Although I understand not a word of his story, its music
and the sacramental avatism of the occasion send all the
rivers of Khasia coursing down my spine. This is poetry, the
marrow, bone and flesh of it; here, in all its knobbly, bardic
majesty, is the kind of poet that we in Wales can only write
history books, a functioning remembrancer of the tribe?

I think now of Nigel and his own poetry, sitting at his 'making table'. He, like the old man in Khasia, gave us the marrow, bone and flesh of poetry and yes, too, in all its knobbly, bardic majesty. And in his prose he gave us Swansea, Gower, Wales, all carefully examined and turned over, like holding a snipe's egg discovered in some secret nest among the rushes. He held it tenderly, might even have touched the speckled rim of it to know its taste, as he once did with a pebble on a Gower beach. In that he was a sensualist, and his poetry can be lush with sensation, and sharp with perception.

Nigel. Poet. Sensualist, exquisitely-elegant fashioner of fine prose, and, through the Encyclopedia, a remembrancer, too, of this small land and its complications, its beauties, myths, histories and stories. But for me, also a teacher, a fine and inspiring writer who could show you the good examples, his good examples of a honed sentence, a well turned phrase, the perfectly choice word in the perfectly right place, rather than proclaim or robotically repeat the specious theories of creative writing as a taught subject. He taught me how to hunt down the right words – the *ensorcelling* song of the curlew, say. He so often claimed the apposite, magical, soaring word. That's why, in my opinion, he was the guv'nor.

In a *Planet* review of Nigel's *Footsore on the Frontier* David Lloyd describes the essays therein as 'the product of a generous spirit and a probing intelligence; open to experience, drawn to detail, careful of abstraction or pretension, inventive in establishing subtle or surprising connections among disparate subjects. It's the product of a writer who wants his words to communicate.'

Yes, his words communicated but they also enraptured, enthralled and oft' times delighted the reader beyond measure. The books aren't just an expression of him, or a version of him, they are him: so, by reading them, with fresh delight, he will never really leave us.

Go well, teacher.

Carmarthen-Swansea train ride

Janet Dubé

The sun over Carmarthen Bay
hung like a fluorescent tomato:
I thought of Idris Davies.

The wallpaper in the waiting room
hung like an abstract of fruit drops;
I thought of John Tripp.

Thinking of someone
to meet my silly mind,
I thought of Nigel Jenkins.

Marwnad
(Nigel Jenkins 1949-2014)

Peter Gruffydd

Gwag yw'r geiriau heno
a'r lleuad allan fel
un llygad i wynebu'r nos.
Clywaf fe es ti'n sydyn,
fel tywyllwch yn disgyn.

You planned your funeral –
Dyna hi? Y diwedd?
Many you inspired will mourn.

I remember we talked and talked,
about words and their vanishings.
And about grey cromlechs, castles
leering with stony gapes from time's
long and obscure attentions.

This news came in a letter –
Word from a friend, warm with sad love,
like your voice which I still hear
sonorous from seas round Wales.

Dyn o galon, a man of heart,
what you left will linger, fruit.
Often you had a helping hand
for mavericks, unacceptables.

And the forgotten: that gift like
finding a rare and delicate
shell which others have passed by,
a fine filigree lit by risen sun.

Dyn a galon, o galon ...

Other titles available from The H'mm Foundation

R.S. Thomas – poet, priest, nationalist – came to dominate the Welsh literary scene in the second half of the twentieth and was nominated for the Nobel Prize for Literature.

Published on the centenary of his birth, these essays show the many ways in which both the man and the poetry inspired affection and admiration in others.

With contributions from:
Gillian Clarke
Fflur Dafydd
Grahame Davies
Gwyneth Lewis
Peter Finch
Jon Gower
Menna Elfyn
Osi Rhys Osmond
Jeff Towns
M. Wynn Thomas
Alex Salmond
Archbishop of Wales Barry Morgan

Encounters with R.S. | £9.99
978-0-9927560-0-0
Edited by John Barnie

Other titles available from The H'mm Foundation

To commemorate the centenary of another major Welsh poet and writer – and another Thomas – 2014 sees the publication of *Encounters with Dylan*, which features essays by academics and aficionados, poets and performers who have variously delighted in and engaged with the work of the self-styled 'Rimbaud of Cwmdonkin Drive'.

With contributions from:
Gary Raymond
D.J. Britton
Guy Masterson
George Tremlett
Steve Groves
Sarah King
Dai George
Sarah Gridley
Horatio Clare
Rachel Trezise
Jeff Towns
Michael Bogdanov
Kaite O'Reilly
Dafydd Elis-Thomas

Encounters with Dylan | £9.99
978-0-9927560-2-4
Edited by Jon Gower

You can buy this title from www.thehmmfoundation.co.uk
also available as an ebook on amazon.co.uk

Encounters with Nigel

.